HOMESCHOOLING
with
GENTLENESS

A Catholic Discovers Unschooling

Cataloging-in-Publication Data:

Andres, Suzie

Homeschooling with gentleness: a Catholic discovers unschooling / Suzie Andres : with a preface by Ralph McInerny. – 1ˢᵗ ed. – Front Royal, Va. : Little Way Books, 2004.

p. ; cm.

ISBN: 0-931888-79-4

1. Home schooling—Religious aspects—Catholic Church. 2. Child rearing—Religious aspects—Catholic Church. 3. Christian life. I. Title.

LC40 .A43 2004   2004103776
371.04/2—dc22   0406

Interior book design by Tom McGraw & William Fahey
Cover design by Ben Hatke

Published in the United States of America by:

Christendom College Press
Front Royal
Virginia

Acknowledgments of permission to use copyrighted materials will be found at the end of this book.

HOMESCHOOLING
with
GENTLENESS

A Catholic Discovers Unschooling

Suzie Andres

With a Preface by Ralph McInerny

LITTLE WAY
BOOKS

Little Way Books takes Nazareth as the measure and model for Christian family life. The editors and authors hope that all our offerings will delight, edify, and assist all parents in achieving the principle goals of the domestic church: to bring its members into deeper and deeper knowledge of the mystery of salvation and the gift of our faith; to encourage each heart to adore the Blessed Trinity through liturgy and familial devotions; to train each person for his vocation by zealously pursuing righteousness and holiness in his daily life.

These books are offered to all Christians, but especially parents, at every stage of spiritual and familial life that they may advance in wisdom and grace, and may advance with the knowledge that this may be accomplished through the most humble acts of charity.

Little Way Books is an imprint of Christendom College Press.

"Do not be afraid any longer, little flock,
For your Father is pleased
To give you the kingdom."
(Luke 12:32)

J.M.J.T.

PRAYER
(said with St. Thérèse)
My God,
If this is not Your will,
I ask You for the grace
not to be able to succeed at it.
But if this is for Your glory,
help me.

DEDICATION
To St. Thérèse of the Child Jesus
and the Holy Face
with gratitude for her intercession.
And to Jon Syren
(July 16, 1965—August 3, 1992)
who taught me by word and example
the true meaning of success.

WITH THANKS
To my husband Tony,
For his patience and love.
To our son Joseph,
For being our guinea pig.
To Dominic the miracle baby,
For bringing back the joy of our youth.
And to MaryAnne,
For just being herself.

CONTENTS

PREFACE

There are not many books on How To Breathe or Walking Made Easy, maybe none at all, but for some reason there are books about home schooling. Home here is the location, not the object of the exercise, of course, so the phrase does not conceal an edifice complex. The idea put forward as innovative, corrective, even as revolutionary is that a child should learn at home! We might as well say that a child should have parents.

The question cannot be one of whether a child should learn at home. Where else does he learn to toddle, speak, go potty and all the rest? Nor is it really a matter of saying that, after a certain period of such parental tutelage, the child should be delivered over to experts who will prepare him for his role in society. It is that assumption, that theirs is merely a task preliminary to the serious one of education, that those engaged in home schooling reject. But even those who do not reject it and deliver their children over to the schools go on willy-nilly teaching their young, doing their homework perhaps. But theirs has now become a secondary and supplementary role.

The alternative to that can send shivers down the spine of those schooled to think that the schools alone know how to teach.

Suzie Andres' wise and witty little book is, as billed, a gentle approach to home schooling. Any reader who comes to this subject with fears will have them quickly allayed by the bright and positive discussion.

You will find here no brief against the compulsory schools. Rather home schooling is seen as the natural way, the basic way, in which children can be taught. Schools of the usual sort are an afterthought. Doubtless some of them still do a tolerable job. Suzie Andres is far more interested in putting before the reader the positive, attractive, practical, fulfilling notion of homeschooling.

Not all who flee the formal schools are concerned with the souls as well as the minds of their children. Suzie Andres speaks to Catholic parents who must see their role as a far more comprehensive one. The Church has always insisted that the parents are the primary educators of their children. This little book spells out the implications of that.

I have been teaching for fifty years at the university level. It is no secret that students enter college now with an oddly skewed formation. They can all operate computers and CD players but they have a shaky hold on their mother tongue, history, that sort of thing. And their knowledge of even the basics of the faith is, to say the least, unsure. A few years ago, young people who had been homeschooled began to enter Notre Dame. The contrast between them and the poor kids who had been hindered by an expensive and allegedly Catholic education could not have been more dramatic. The difference was somewhat like that between kids from a loving home and orphans.

When I first met Suzie Andres, her intention was to take a doctorate and devote her life, as her husband has, to college teaching. Having children enlarged and redirected her ambitions. Just about anyone can teach college; only a parent can home school. Chesterton said that husbands are specialists and mothers are universalists, because they have to be all things to their children. That was written a century ago. It is encouraging to see Suzie and so many other young mothers, helped of course by their specialist husbands, exuberantly and joyously enjoying the full benefits of being a parent.

Ralph McInerny
University of Notre Dame

IS THIS BOOK FOR YOU?

My husband is considered a prudent man by those who know him, and I have just asked for his blessing in the writing of this book. His response was, "Sure, you can write it; just don't get carried away." To you, dear reader, I extend the advice, and thus begin by giving you permission: "Sure, you can read it; just don't get carried away." Before you make any big decisions about implementing the ideas that follow, get your spouse's blessing too.

      I am writing this book for myself, and maybe for you too. I have homeschooled my thirteen year old son for the last seven years, and throughout that time (and long before that time) I have been questioning myself and my husband about what in the world we are doing. Like many another Catholic homeschooling mother I have wondered if my son would learn to read (he did), do basic math (he did), express himself coherently (he can), get along with other children and adults (he does), and last but not least, embrace his Catholic faith (he has; phew!). Despite all my worries, fears, and unused curriculum purchases, Joseph has done just fine. In fact, only today we completed seventh grade, and held our typical end-of-the-year ceremony. It went something like this:

MOM: Well, if you do these math problems, I guess you can be done for the year.

SON: Okay.

MOM: Well, I think so. Is there something I'm forgetting?

SON: Um . . . yeah, religion. . . . Thank You Jesus that we are finishing!

MOM: Okay, let me know when you've done the problems.

. . . about half an hour later . . .

SON: Okay, I'm done.

MOM: Let's see . . . uh-huh . . . you've done them. Great! Congratulations! You've finished seventh grade.

Next, the "ceremony": Mom, smiling, shakes son's hand. Dad walks in as Mom attempts to hug son; she tells Dad the good news and announces that son is now an eighth grader. Dad is more interested in noticing that son is almost Mom's height. Then follows an overdue height-measuring-session, which parents are more interested in than son—who is already interested in something else.

This scene gives you a glimpse into our life. Note that what I call a "traditional ceremony" has no crafts, no cooking, not much at all. The "curriculum" we needed to complete was pretty minimal, and the day on which we finished was somewhat arbitrary. If you are highly motivated, thrive on structure and love to fill the official role of teacher, this might not be the book for you.

My primary motive in writing is to clear up some things for myself, get them down on paper, and be able to re-read them when necessary. But I am also writing to share with others the fruits of my experience, prayer, extensive reading, and countless conversations with the wise husband mentioned above. If there are other parents who are homeschooling while striving to eradicate, rather than cement, their tendencies toward perfectionism, a success-oriented outlook, and the modern do-it-all/have-it-all ideal, I write for them also.

My hope is that this book will present a simple explanation of and Catholic defense for an extremely relaxed approach to homeschooling. Over the years my own family has been cultivating a style which has culminated in what my husband and I refer to as "Catholic unschooling." I am not writing to recommend this approach to all Catholic homeschooling families. Rather, I am writing about what works for us, and what I suspect will work for some others. In articulating my own solution to the question of how to homeschool, I offer an alternative method to both the popular classical curriculum model of homeschooling, and the textbook or "school at home" model. But please understand that I am proposing and defending as Catholic *one particular way among many*. I consider it a gentle way, a way suited to little souls, and an easy way. I do not consider it the only way, or the best way for everyone. It is the best way for us, and if it sounds like it might be the best way for you, then I urge you to keep reading and consider giving it a try.

Front Royal
May 26, 2003
Feast of St. Philip Neri

PART ONE:
UNSCHOOLING

CHAPTER ONE:
HOW WE CAME TO UNSCHOOL

A voice I did not know said to me: "I freed your
shoulder from the burden; your hands were freed
from the load. You called in distress and I saved
you. . . . Open wide your mouth and I will fill it."
(from Psalm 81)

What We Have Read

In some ways this is a book about books. Our reading has greatly
influenced our homeschooling, and so an explanation of how we
homeschool must start—for us—with an explanation of what we
have read.

My husband Tony remembers reading Mary Kay Clark's book
Catholic Homeschooling when our older son was a toddler. We were
very impressed with her thesis that schools are not good for children, and that homeschooling is the way to go.

The next important book to influence our thought was Susan Schaeffer McCauley's *For the Children's Sake*. In this marvelous
book Mrs. McCauley presents the educational philosophy of Charlotte Mason, an Englishwoman who died in 1923. Charlotte Mason, according to Mrs. McCauley, based her work on the central
tenet that education must be for the children's sake. While this
point may seem obvious, it gave us the reason why the average
school is not good for children. Homeschooling is far superior to
compulsory schooling because the former can keep the child's wel-
fare at the forefront, while the latter generally sacrifices the good
of the individual child for some other nebulous good.

The final step in our homeschooling journey, and the one
which marked our conscious conversion to unschooling, came with
our introduction to the work of John Holt. Holt was an educator

and writer who died in 1985, leaving behind him eleven books and the first homeschooling magazine, *Growing Without Schooling*, which he had founded in 1977. We uncovered in Holt's books the recurrent theme that children have a natural inclination and ability to learn, and that thus we can trust them to follow their desires and learn what they need to know. This principle resonated with us, for it was a modern expression of Aristotle's profound insight that all men desire to know, as an end, and that consequently it is natural and fulfilling for them to learn. Holt's emphasis on children's wonder, eagerness to learn, and joy in life and learning also recalled the spirit of St. Thérèse. In particular, his support of freedom and love in place of fear-inspiring compulsion in our guidance of children is reminiscent of her admission: "My nature was such that fear made me recoil; with love not only did I advance, I actually flew" (*Story of a Soul*, p. 174).

What We Have Done

Around the time of our reading Mary Kay Clark's book and Susan Schaeffer McCauley's, we determined we would homeschool our son Joseph. As he reached the very social age of four, however, I began to panic and grow weary at the mere thought of homeschooling. Hence we enrolled him in the nearest attractive looking pre-K program, and I breathed a sigh of relief. The school went through twelfth grade and had a good reputation; my worries were over.

Fortunately, it didn't work out as I had hoped. Due to some differences with the teachers, we pulled Joseph out of this school the day before what would have been his second year there. Just as quickly we enrolled him in a tiny new Catholic enterprise which would begin the school year two days later. Once again I planned on avoiding homeschooling by keeping him in the second school until college. Alas, and thanks be to God, again my plans were foiled. While we enjoyed the friendships formed there, the growing pains and parental commitment required by such a young institution were too much for me.

At the end of Joseph's second year of school, when he was just six years old, I assessed our school experience, asked myself, "Well, why not? It need only be for a year if it doesn't work, " and told my husband I was ready to try homeschooling Joseph for first grade. This time Tony breathed a sigh of relief, graciously refrained from saying anything like "I told you so," and gave me his full support.

The first thing I did was order a boxed curriculum, which literally came in a box with even the pencils and paper included. Incidentally, this was from the Calvert School in Baltimore, Maryland. Our use of their extremely high-quality materials and well-organized lesson plans lasted maybe four days (I am probably exaggerating; in fact, it was most likely three days)! I apologized to my husband for wasting money, but this carefully orchestrated curriculum was not working out. He generously told me the money was not wasted, since the purchase had given me the courage to begin. With such an introduction to homeschooling in practice, perhaps we should have seen the writing on the wall . . .

I had re-read *For the Children's Sake*, and we agreed with Mrs. McCauley and Charlotte Mason that children should spend only a bit of the day doing desk work, with ample time left to play freely and enjoy the outdoors. Accordingly, I spent small amounts of time with Joseph doing pages in workbooks, much larger chunks of time reading aloud, and we let him use most of his time playing, inside and out.

First grade passed. Joseph learned to read, and it seemed very natural. Having done some phonics workbooks in his previous two schools, and having listened to much reading aloud, he sat on the couch with me and slowly sounded out two beginning readers, a couple of pages at a time. Suddenly, Joseph was able to read on his own. It seemed to us that we played a very minor role in that transition, which really hinged on his being ready.

Second and third grades passed uneventfully, with a small failed foray into Suzuki violin. The teacher was excellent, the method seemed wonderful, yet after two or three short months, Joseph and I knew it was not for us. Another attempt at cultural enrichment went more smoothly: for several months a friend of mine spent an hour a week teaching Joseph a few French songs and games. Although we never continued with the French, Joseph, Kathleen and I enjoyed the diversion that their classes provided.

For our serious schoolwork, we depended on what I dubbed "the K-mart curriculum." This consisted of a few inexpensive workbooks for our minimal written work at the dining room table. Mostly, Joseph spent hours with his Lego sets, his neighborhood friends, and many good books.

In the summers between school years, I have always enjoyed reading a lot about homeschooling, talking with Tony about our goals and methods, and planning for the upcoming academic year. Around this time I read in depth about Charlotte Mason's method, and planned to integrate more of her ideas in our fourth grade. These included nature study and nature journaling, narration (a child's re-telling) using Aesop's fables, and sustained contact with great music and art. Somehow, despite all my plans, fourth grade looked a lot like third, second, and first. I consoled myself that at least we had obtained a year long pass to nearby Skyline Drive in Shenandoah National Park, for our nature study.

For fifth grade we returned to a curriculum provider (Sonlight), which placed a heavy emphasis on learning history through literature. Joseph had been doing this for the last three or four years on his own—I supplied the books, he devoured them—so we were easily sold on the idea. This company marketed a fifth grade curriculum which focused on developing a missionary spirit by reading about the non-Western, largely non-Christian parts of the world. We thoroughly enjoyed many of their books and their emphasis on the parent reading aloud to the child, but somehow our year ended up, once again, looking like the previous years. Joseph would do a minimum of seat-work, namely math and handwriting, we would read a lot together and alone, and he would play by himself and with friends for much of the day.

The summer after fifth grade I read *How Children Fail* and *How Children Learn*, and finally, *Learning All the Time* by John Holt. As usual, I read out loud to Tony many passages that especially resonated with me, and we talked and talked and talked. We realized that the homeschooling we had been doing with Joseph looked very similar to what is called unschooling. More importantly, with the help of John Holt we came to understand what it means for education to be "for the children's sake."

Sixth grade with Joseph resembled the previous years, but I was much more relaxed about the small amount of traditional school work we did. The next summer I bought a set of back issues of John Holt's magazine *Growing Without Schooling* (which unfortunately ceased publication in the year 2001). I enjoyed the hundreds of stories by families who wrote in telling about how they lived and learned. I was amazed at the wide-ranging interests of the children in these families, and impressed by the degree of expertise which they commonly achieved by freely pursuing such interests. Again, I felt quite encouraged to continue along the path we had been following.

The last discovery we made was the work of John Taylor Gatto. In that same summer I bought books by this former New York City and New York State Teacher of the Year, and read the letter he wrote to *The Wall Street Journal* to announce his resignation after twenty-five years in the public school system. Tony and I were fascinated by his history and critique of compulsory schooling. We came full circle to an understanding of why Mary Kay Clark was right that schools are not good places for children. Gatto convincingly argues that the school system we have was not designed for the children's sake, and cannot be reformed for their sake.

When my husband and I consider what we have learned since we first thought about homeschooling, we realize that our reading of these important books, our frequent conversations, and our experience with Joseph have all led us in one direction: toward unschooling. Seventh grade had less required work than ever, which was partly due to our agreement with John Holt's ideas, and partly due to the arrival of our second child, Dominic. The year flew by; our days held a little bit of math, a little bit of piano, and a lot of learning how to make a baby laugh.

As I write, it is the summer before eighth grade. I look forward to spending time in these next three months reading more of John Holt's books, and being encouraged by more old issues of *Growing Without Schooling*. I am also writing this book of my own, because it seems the right time to spell out our conclusions. Tony has reassured me over and over that Catholic unschooling makes sense, and his defense is not long or difficult.

In the pages that follow, I will articulate the reasons for unschooling, and show that Catholics can use this approach without fear of failing their children. I have discovered, however, that anxiety is the constant companion of homeschooling mothers, and our fears are not so easily vanquished. And so I will also write about learning to trust nature and God, in order to find freedom and peace in our parenting. Since our unschooling has depended so heavily on reading, I will conclude by extolling the virtues of books as friends. Lastly, in order to help the reader meet our best friends among the books, I will append lists of the books we have most enjoyed. For the children's sake, I hope others will find something of use in what I write.

CHAPTER TWO:
WHAT IS UNSCHOOLING
AND WHY DOES IT MAKE SENSE?

What Unschooling Is

So far I have spoken loosely of unschooling, but in order to understand why it works, and how Catholics can be unschoolers, we will need to be clear about what we mean by the term "unschooling." In the *Homeschooling Handbook*, Mary Griffith gives a helpful introduction to unschooling, explaining both the origin and current use of the word. She writes:

> Educator John Holt wrote extensively about school reform in the 1960's, but by the late 1970's he had concluded that no reform would make schools effective places for children to learn. Although he originally proposed the word "unschooling" simply as a more satisfactory alternative to "homeschooling," unschooling now generally refers to a specific style of homeschooling, in which learning is not separated from living, and children learn mainly by following their own interests. Children learn best, he argued, not by being taught, but by being a part of the world, free to explore what most interests them, by having their questions answered as they ask them, and by being treated with respect rather than condescension. (pp. 56-57)

While this description provides us with an understanding of what was and is meant by unschooling generally, we need to be more specific in order to avoid ambiguity. In short, what we need is a formal definition of unschooling. As I will explain in the next

chapter, a definition of this word is hard to find. After much delib-
eration and a few consultations with my philosopher husband, I
have come up with the following, which will serve as our definition
throughout this book:

> Unschooling is a form of education in which the child is trusted
> to be the primary agent in learning what he needs to know to
> lead him to happiness.

Bear with me as I clarify the parts of this definition, and then
we will be able to continue our discussion with less likelihood of
confusion.

First, "form of education," refers in particular to academic
education, not to moral education. Since, however, "academic
education" seems to limit the unschooler to reading, writing, and
arithmetic, I hesitate to add that qualifier to our definition. Those
who educate their children at home usually include more in their
homeschool than a typical school's subjects. They come to see
homeschooling as education which encompasses such areas as
manners and household management, which might not be considered academic. Nonetheless, I want to be clear that I am not proposing unschooling as a form of moral education, because I do not
want to imply that unschooling makes the child the primary agent
in his own moral upbringing.

Next, "the child is trusted": those who are trusting the child
are his parents. They are trusting him to be the primary agent in
his learning, but this does not amount to neglect on their part.
The parents assume the role of secondary agents, meaning that
they do not forsake their duties in their child's education, but rather
they recognize and honor his natural ability to learn. They do not
ignore the child, or refuse to guide him. Instead they allow him a
leading role in his education, placing more emphasis on his learning than on their teaching.

To those familiar with the thought of Maria Montessori, these ideas about trusting the child will not be entirely new. This essential aspect of unschooling is also similar to the principle of "masterly inactivity" employed by Charlotte Mason. Penny Gardner writes in her *Charlotte Mason Study Guide*:

> This means not stepping in, taking initiative away from the child. Let the child reap the natural consequences of his actions. She [Charlotte Mason] said, "We are very tenacious of the dignity and originality of our children . . . . Do not take too much upon ourselves, but leave time and scope for the workings of Nature and of a higher Power than Nature herself . . . . The art of standing aside to let a child develop the relations proper to him is the fine art of education. (p. 2)

Finally, let us consider that the end of unschooling is the end of all education: that is, the acquisition of knowledge and skills. Because unschooling, like all homeschooling, is for the child's sake, the knowledge and skills proposed are not accidental; they are those which the child needs to become truly happy.

This, then, is what we mean by unschooling. What differentiates it from schooling is that in unschooling the knowledge and skills which make up the education are for the child's sake, and are learned for the sake of his happiness. Schools could also have this end, but too often they don't. The further distinction which separates unschooling from other methods of homeschooling is the emphasis on trusting the child to be the primary agent of his education. While other approaches tend to focus on the teaching done by the parent, unschooling concentrates on the learning done by the student. Again, this emphasis is not wholly unique to unschooling; one finds it also in the Montessori and Charlotte Mason methods. I think, however, that unschooling takes this principle farther than either of the other methods do.

Why Unschooling Makes Sense

All Men by Nature Desire to Know

There are several reasons why unschooling, as we have defined it, makes sense. I touched on the first and most important reason in the last chapter, namely, that children have a natural desire and inclination to learn. Parents of small children observe this natural curiosity constantly. Its intensity can even be annoying, as when a toddler persists in exploring a prohibited area of the house, or when a four year old's refrain of "But why Mommy?" seems endless. We are so used to seeing this interest in the world squelched when children begin formal schooling that we are too often blasé about their wonder's unnatural end. We come to expect that children will be bored by academics and resistant to learning, forgetting that up until the age of five or six they were full of enthusiasm and in awe of the whole world opening before them.

Anyone can realize that man has an innate fundamental desire to learn, by thinking over his own experience and by observing children. As I have said, John Holt was the writer who reminded me of this truth. He never tired of repeating that children are natural, eager, and able learners. In *How Children Learn*, he wrote, "What I am trying to say about education rests on a belief that, though there is much evidence to support it, I cannot prove, and that may never be proved. Call it faith. This faith is that man is by nature a learning animal. Birds fly, fish swim; man thinks and learns" (p. 293). Holt expands on this principle in the last essay of his last book, *Learning All the Time*. The essay is called "Every Waking Hour," and begins:

> Among the many things I have learned about children, learned by many, many years of hanging out with them, watching carefully what they do, and thinking about it, is that children are natural learners.

The one thing we can be sure of, or surest of, is that children have a passionate desire to understand as much of the world as they can, even what they cannot see and touch, and as far as possible to acquire some kind of skill, competence, and control in it and over it. Now this desire, this need to understand the world and be able to do things in it, the things the big people do, is so strong that we could properly call it biological. It is every bit as strong as the need for food, for warmth, for shelter, for comfort, for sleep, for love. In fact, I think a strong case could be made that it might be stronger than any of these.

A hungry child, even a tiny baby who experiences hunger as real pain, will stop eating or nursing or drinking if something interesting happens, because that little child wants to see what it is. This curiosity, this desire to make some kind of sense out of things, goes right to the heart of the kind of creatures that we are. (pp. 159-160)

Almost 2,500 years ago, Aristotle made this same point in the first paragraph of the *Metaphysics*. There we read:

All men by nature desire to know. An indication of this is the delight we take in our senses; for even apart from their usefulness they are loved for themselves; and above all others the sense of sight. For not only with a view to action, but even when we are not going to do anything, we prefer seeing (one might say) to everything else. The reason is that this, most of all the senses, makes us know and brings to light many differences between things. (980a)

One obstacle we encounter in our thought about education is that while we can easily see this trait in children if we take the time to observe them, our imaginations often play tricks on us. When we think of formal learning, we often envision children as restless and uninterested participants. This image may grow out of our own memories of the seemingly endless, achingly boring hours spent in school desks. We then project our experience onto the children in our charge, imagining that they too will be reluctant learners.

Reading John Holt is a great antidote to our fears. In the following beautiful passage, with which he concludes the revised edition of *How Children Learn*, Holt vividly portrays this principle of the child's natural inclination to learn. His poetic descriptions can help us, by filling our imaginations with accurate pictures of children happily at work in learning about the world. He writes:

What is lovely about children is that they can make such a production, such a big deal, out of everything, or nothing. From my office I see many families walking down Boylston Street with their little children. The adults plod along, the children twirl, leap, skip, run now to this side and now to that, look for things to step or jump over or walk along or around, climb on anything that can be climbed . . . . All that energy and foolishness, all that curiosity, questions, talk, all those fierce passions, inconsolable sorrows, immoderate joys, seem to many a nuisance to be endured, if not a disease to be cured. To me they are a national asset, a treasure beyond price, more necessary to our health and our very survival than any oil or uranium or—name what you will.

One day in the Public Garden I see, on a small patch of grass under some trees, a father and a two-year-old girl. The father is lying down; the little girl runs everywhere. What joy to run! Suddenly she stops, looks intently at the ground, bends down, picks something up. A twig! A pebble! She stands up, runs again, sees a pigeon, chases it, suddenly stops and looks up into the sunlit trees, seeing what?—perhaps a squirrel, perhaps a bird, perhaps just the shape and colors of the leaves in the sun. Then she bends down, finds something else, picks it up, examines it. A leaf! Another miracle!

Gears, twigs, leaves, little children love the world. That is why they are so good at learning about it. For it is love, not tricks and techniques of thought, that lies at the heart of all true learning. Can we bring ourselves to let children learn and grow through that love? (pp. 302-303)

Holt is here writing about young children, but the reader may wonder to what extent we can expect older children to exhibit their natural love of learning, especially when it comes to the typical academic subjects. Again, we should not underestimate the damage that compulsory schooling has done. School-aged children often become bored by repetitive seat work and bland textbooks. Too much teaching can result in the lack of interest in learning we see in such children. And yet do you remember the excitement you felt in the classrooms of your youth when someone brought in a pet lizard or hamster? Life had crept back into the classroom! The sparkle of curiosity reappeared in the children's eyes, and everyone felt a renewed interest in the world . . . . When we consider school in light of these memories, our question changes from "Will older children learn?" to "Will they learn when their environment is dull and lifeless?" That is a different question, and indicates the role of parents as secondary agents in their kids' education, responsible for providing the children with a nurturing home life and a healthy amount of access to the world.

John Holt became an advocate of homeschooling after giving up on reforming schools, where he had taught for several years. His experience confirms our conjecture that the desire to learn can be suppressed by stale schooling or even by too much teaching, however well-intended. In the essay "Every Waking Hour," from which we quoted above, Holt continues:

> Children are not only extremely good at learning; they are much better at it than we are. As a teacher, it took me a long time to find this out. I was an ingenious and resourceful teacher, clever about thinking up lesson plans and demonstrations and motivating devices and all of that acamaracus. And I only very slowly and painfully—believe me, painfully—learned that when I started teaching less, the children started learning more.
>
> I can sum up in five to seven words what I eventually learned as a teacher. The seven-word version is: Learning is not the product of teaching. The five-word version is: Teaching does not make learning. As I mentioned before, organized education operates on the assumption that children learn only when and only what and only because we teach them. This is not true. (p. 160)

We have seen then, with the help of John Holt and the wisdom of Aristotle, that learning is natural to man. This is the first
reason that unschooling makes sense. Because the desire to know
is a deep-seated part of our nature, children can be trusted to pursue knowledge. Hence they can become primary agents in their
education, and within a nurturing friendly environment they will
learn.

What will they learn? While the answer depends somewhat
on their particular surroundings and their interests, we can trust
that they will learn the traditional academic subjects such as reading, writing and arithmetic. The second and third reasons that
unschooling makes sense are that what we call "the basics" are of
intrinsic interest to children, and these "subjects" are not hard to
learn.

The Basics Are Interesting

As Holt told us above, children want to be like big people. If they
see the adults around them reading, writing, and using math in
daily life, they will realize the importance of these pursuits. I remember as a child imitating my mom by scribbling rows of "writing" that were really just wavy lines. But they looked to me like
what she did, and I wanted to be big and write too. We see countless examples of this whenever children are around grown-ups. My
husband remembers that his boredom with school was partly due
to its obvious artificiality. No adults he knew did book reports or
made dioramas, so those things were unimportant and uninterest-
ing to him. On the other hand, his parents read a lot; books were
obviously useful tools and enjoyable objects to them, and an aware-
ness of this made him value books as well. His father knew about
cars, his mother was involved in politics; hence, cars and politics
were things Tony loved and wanted to know all about.

We can draw the conclusion that reading, writing and arithmetic, if important to us, are going to be of interest to our children.

It is also likely that even without our example, children would gravitate toward learning these intrinsically interesting things, but with our example, it is a sure thing.

The Basics Are Not Hard To Learn

But will they be able to learn these things? Don't we need to step in and help them to master such complex tasks? John Holt has a lot to say in response to these concerns. His book *Learning All the Time* features chapters with titles such as "Reading and Writing," "At Home with Numbers," and "Young Children as Research Scientists." I highly recommend this book, for in it Holt shows "how children learn to read and write and count at home—with very little or no teaching" (p. xv). His thesis is:

> That children, without being coerced or manipulated, or being put in exotic, specially prepared environments, or having their thinking planned and ordered for them, can, will, and do pick up from the world around them important information about what we call the Basics. (p. xv)

Perhaps it is enough for our purposes to return to our own experiences. I personally know, or have heard of, many children who learned to read with a minimum of adult involvement. Family members told these kids the names of the different letters, and taught the sounds of the letters when the children asked. Then by some quiet invisible process, the child began putting the sounds together when he saw the letters, and eureka! Another reader was born.

In *Learning All the Time*, John Holt explains a fascinating truth about learning to read, and gives some characteristic advice about "teaching" reading. He writes in the essay, "Sensible Phonics":

> The fact is that there are only two general ideas that one needs to grasp in order to be able to read a phonic language like

English (or French, German, and Italian, as opposed to, say, Chinese): (1) written letters stand for spoken sounds; (2) the order of the letters on the page, from our left to our right, corresponds to the order in time of the spoken sounds.

It is not necessary for children to be able to say these rules in order to understand and be able to use them. Nor is it a good idea to try to teach them these rules by saying and then explaining them. The way to teach them—that is if you insist on teaching them—is to demonstrate it through very simple and clear examples. (p. 23)

Suffice it to say that Holt, in this book and elsewhere, convincingly makes the case that learning the basics is not difficult. He does add, though, that learning these and other things can be made difficult by over-zealous teaching.

The Importance of Readiness in Learning

Which brings us to another reason for unschooling. By planning out a child's curriculum for him, a parent runs the risk of trying to teach things to the child before the child is ready.

Perhaps the most common occurrence of this urge to hurry the child is in the realm of reading. If a homeschooling mother manages to suppress her fear that her child will *never* learn to read, she is still plagued by the concern that he won't learn to read when he *should*, that is, by the time it is "normal" for all children to know how to read. For some parents this magic age is five, for others it is six, and for the most relaxed parents, the child has until age seven to master reading. If the child is slow to learn at these ages, parents have been conditioned to panic that maybe the problem is an underlying "learning disability."

As we saw in the previous pages, John Holt has done us a great service by explaining that it is not hard, in itself, to learn to read. The other early pioneers of the homeschooling movement, Raymond and Dorothy Moore, made their mark with the theory "better late than early." They were convinced, along with John

Holt, that learning disablilities, dyslexia, and the like, are often merely the result of our "rushing our little ones into school too early, or . . . otherwise pressuring them" (*Home Style Teaching*, p. 75).

While John Holt relied on his own experiences with children, the Moores analyzed over 8,000 childhood studies to develop and confirm their opinions on education. In their book *Home Style Teaching* they explain the importance of readiness.

> Two principles which child development research clearly supports are *first*, that the success a child will achieve in learning any particular skill is dependent upon his maturity—his mental, physical, and emotional readiness; and *second*, that the child becomes competent in a much shorter time when he is older than when he is younger. Many of you have watched these principles operate in your own families. You can work very hard to teach a child a certain skill at an early age, such as crawling up the stairs. But if you just wait a while he will learn it largely by himself. This principle operates in the development of coordination, reason, math, and even reading. It seems evident that we should try to discover more about what children really need instead of imposing adult standards on them; then move ahead to assist by being good examples and responders. In other words, read *to* them and *with* them. (p. 76)

The Moore's argument in favor of waiting for readiness is completed by their fascinating discovery that, in the end, the age at which a skill is learned does not determine a child's later progress or ability. For example, children who learn to read "late" (say at the age of nine or ten) can read as well as those who learned "early" (say at the age of four or five) within a very short time. Comparing children whose parents wait for readiness with children whose parents ignore readiness in favor of producing geniuses, the Moores write:

> Usually these naturally ready children are reading far ahead of their peers after a few months of instruction. And they have done this without the risk of burnout, anxiety, frustration, dys-

lexia, and neurosis, which many of these rushed children experience. (pp. 148-149)

Never having been energetic enough to try to produce a genius, in the past I have merely worked anxiously to keep Joseph near what I consider the necessary average math development. (After your child learns to read, you relax for fifteen minutes and then begin to panic over his math abilities!) I remember in particular our struggle with long division. As I will explain later in this book, I have not had much success teaching Joseph new concepts. When I attempted to teach long division, he and I became so frustrated that we finally gave up, but only after I bullishly succeeded in pushing him through several problems. This was over the course of the last weeks of fifth grade, and we were both grateful for the summer break. When we began sixth grade, we found that Joseph was somehow ready for long division, and picked it up with ease.

This sequence was repeated in other endeavors, but avoided on the occasions when Tony and I could wait for Joseph's own initiative to show that he was more than ready to learn a new skill. Two examples of quick learning when Joseph was ready come to mind: when he was six he learned to tie his shoes in one three minute "lesson," and at seven he learned to ride his bike without training wheels on the first try. In both these instances, we did not consciously wait for Joseph to be ready, but just didn't think to teach him until he was past ready! The happy result was Joseph learning the skills easily and quickly.

The dangers of teaching a subject or skill to a child who is not disposed to learn it are primarily two: at best, the teacher is wasting the child's time, which he could be using to investigate other matters; but at its worst, premature teaching will set up obstacles to later learning, either because the child is intimidated by what seems so hard, or because he adopts confused notions about the particular subject.

The Argument for Unschooling

From the reasons we have examined, we can compose an argument in defense of unschooling. Unschooling, which is education characterized by trusting the child to learn, makes sense because what the child needs to learn is not hard to learn in itself. Furthermore, he has a natural inclination and ability to learn it, as well as a strong desire to imitate his parents: to know the things they know, and to do the things they do. Finally, unschooling makes sense because it recognizes the student as the primary agent of his education, and thus helps parents to avoid over-teaching and teaching before the child is ready.

There are many advantages to unschooling, in addition to the reasons we have given thus far. Some of these will surface as we proceed. For now, we have a definition of unschooling and an argument that it makes sense. It is time to see what unschooling families look like, and then we will ask if any such unschooling family can be Catholic.

CHAPTER THREE:
WHAT UNSCHOOLING LOOKS LIKE

What Unschooling Doesn't Look Like

In the imaginations of many homeschoolers, the word "unschooling" conjures up one of two pictures. The first is the picture of a family whose children are allowed to do whatever they choose during "school" hours. Fulfilling every parent's worst fears, the kids spend the majority of their time watching television, playing computer games, and reading comic books, if they have learned to read at all. The second image shows a family whose parents, though naturally desiring to guide their children's education, are afraid of hampering their children's freedom. These parents feel guilty directing their children (hampering their freedom), and yet feel equally guilty not directing their children (neglecting their education). The parents skulk around, surreptitiously placing enriching reading materials about the house, while constantly on the lookout for "teachable moments" in order to seize frantically on the children's every interest.

Having considered what unschooling is and the reasons it makes sense, we are in a good position to combat the errors contained in such caricatures. As we formulate our own image of what an unschooling family might look like in action, we can begin by saying that it need not look like the families just described.

First, we saw that children are curious, and eager to learn about the world around them. For safety's sake, my husband and I prefer not to have free access to television, computer games, and the internet in our home. In this way we ensure that the temptation to become couch potatoes will not overcome us in our weaker moments. But it is unlikely that other unschooling families who do allow television and computer use for their children would degenerate into the passive characters outlined above. As we stated in the last chapter, children want to know how to do the things their parents do; if the parents are engaged in work and leisure activities in sight or hearing of the kids, the family will likely end up pursuing some of these together. A family that takes the trouble to keep children out of the compulsory school system is not likely to be a family that spends all its time watching television! (In my reading about unschooling families, I have come across stories in which the children needed time to unwind and "deschool" after they left traditional schools. Even in these situations, when the kids seem to do nothing for a time, they then emerge from their malaise and begin again to enjoy life and learning, often investigating new areas of interest.)

Next, in our definition of unschooling we implied that the parents are secondary agents of their children's education. Parents who understand that children have a natural inclination and ability to learn, and who realize the beauty and attraction of the created world, will not feel a desperate need to promote every passing interest of their children. At the same time, a healthy appreciation of their role as facilitators and guides for their children will conquer most parents' fears of being overbearing in their direction of the children's education. Contrary to popular opinion, informed unschooling parents can strike a balance between too much teaching and a total hands-off approach.

Having seen what unschooling doesn't look like, we are ready to sketch a more hopeful scenario of the unschooling family, and what it does look like.

What Unschooling Looks Like

The books and magazines I have read about unschooling commonly avoid giving a definition of it. Instead, the authors write that unschooling means different things to different families. At first I was both confused and annoyed by this approach, but I have come to understand the authors' reluctance to give a definition, and their substitution of quotations from lots of particular families about "what unschooling means to us." On the one hand, even a carefully crafted definition could alienate some readers, who would respond that this doesn't capture what they do, or how they see themselves. On the other hand, acknowledging the diverse activities and concerns of different unschooling families recognizes the actual variation in those who call themselves unschoolers.

Such books have spurred me on to carefully define unschooling, and this effort has helped me to clarify what seems essential about it, and what separates unschooling from schooling and homeschooling. As I work out "what unschooling looks like," I realize that now there must be a general character to my account, precisely where the other books give many particular instances. The truth is that there is not one picture of the typical unschooling family. The size of the family, the temperaments of family members, the work and hobbies of the parents, the area in which they live with access to city or country life, their friends and neighbors and relatives, the energy level of kids and parents; all these will play a part in how each unschooling family learns together. Since unschooling allows freedom in the scope and sequence of learning, the factors listed (and many more) will determine different directions for and appearances of unschooling families.

Consequently our explanation of what unschooling looks like will not paint a detailed portrait of the typical unschooling family. Instead, we will return to the writings of John Holt for a rough sketch of what unschooling parents and children do, and how they learn together. With his help, we can see what it means—in practice—to trust children, and how parents can help them to be the primary agents in their own education.

John Holt on What Unschooling Looks Like

Let's start with two excerpts from Holt's book *Teach Your Own*. These are taken from the chapter "Common Objections to Homeschooling." In the first passage, Holt describes what the relationship between unschooling parents and children looks like. In the second passage, he describes what kinds of things unschooling families will do together. He writes:

> We can sum up very quickly what people need to teach their own children. First of all, they have to like them, enjoy their company, their physical presence, their energy, foolishness, and passion. They have to enjoy all their talk and questions, and enjoy equally trying to answer those questions. They have to think of their children as friends, indeed very close friends, have to feel happier when they are near and miss them when they are away. They have to trust them as people, respect their fragile dignity, treat them with courtesy, take them seriously. They have to feel in their own hearts some of their children's wonder, curiosity, and excitement about the world. And they have to have enough confidence in themselves, skepticism about experts, and willingness to be different from most people, to take on themselves the responsibility for their children's learning. But that is about all that parents need. (p. 46)

> Children don't need, don't want, and couldn't stand six hours of teaching a day, even if parents wanted to do that much. To help them find out about the world doesn't take that much adult input. Most of what they need, parents have been giving them since they were born. As I have said, they need access. They need a chance, sometimes, for honest, serious, unhurried talk; or sometimes, for joking, play, and foolishness; or sometimes, for tenderness, sympathy, and comfort. They need, much of the time, to share your life, or at least, not to feel shut out of it, in short, to go some of the places you go, see and do some of the things that interest you, get to know some of your friends, find out what you did when you were little and

before they were born. They need to have their questions answered, or at least heard and attended to—if you don't know, say "I don't know." They need to know more and more adults whose main work in life is not taking care of kids [i.e. who are not schoolteachers]. They need some friends their own age, but not dozens of them; two or three, at most half a dozen, is as many real friends as any child can have at one time. Perhaps above all, they need a lot of privacy, solitude, calm, times when there's nothing to do. (p. 48)

In the book *Learning All the Time*, Holt has a section entitled "What Parents Can Do." In the following paragraphs he continues to describe what unschooling looks like, explaining in more detail how unschooling parents will help their children learn by giving them access to the world. Holt comments:

We have road maps of the world, not just real road maps, but various mental road maps of the world around us. What adults can do for children is to make more and more of that world and the people in it accessible and transparent to them. The key word is access: to people, places, experiences, the places where we work, other places we go—cities, countries, streets, buildings. We can also make available tools, books, records, toys, and other resources. On the whole, kids are more interested in the things that adults really use than in the little things we buy especially for them. I mean, anyone who has seen little kids in the kitchen knows that they would rather play with the pots and pans than anything made by Fisher-Price or Lego or name whomever you will. (p. 127)

Many young children do indeed need to be introduced to tasks and activities that take time, concentration, effort, and skill. But this isn't a matter of "giving" harder tasks and making the child persist until he or she is finished. In such situations the controlling factor is the will of the adult, not, as it should be, the requirements of the task. Instead, what young children need is the opportunity to see older children and adults choosing and undertaking various tasks and working on them over a period of time until they are completed. Children need to get some sense of the processes by which good work is done. The only way they can learn how much time and effort it takes to build, say, a table, is to be able to see someone building a table, from start to finish. Or painting a picture. Or repairing a bicycle, or writing a story, or whatever it may be . . . . Children need to see things done well. Cooking, and especially baking, where things change their texture and shape (and taste yummy), are skills that children might like to take part in. Typing might be another, and to either or both of these could be added bookmaking and bookbinding. These are crafts that children could take part in from beginning to end. Skilled drawing and painting or woodworking might be others.

Adults must use the skills they have where children can see them. In the unlikely event that they have no skills to speak of, they should learn some, and let the children see them learning, even if only as simple a thing as touch typing. They should invite children to join them in using these skills. In this way children can be slowly drawn, at higher and higher levels of energy, commitment, and skill, into more and more serious and worthwhile adult activities. (pp. 130-131)

We see from the above quotations that the parents and children in unschooling families spend time together, work, play, and talk together. But what about more obvious cases of teaching and learning? Will we see unschooling parents teaching their children, and if so, how will they go about it? In *Learning All the Time* there is a short essay called "Teaching as a Natural Science." Here Holt describes what teaching should look like in the unschooling family. He writes:

Like a naturalist, an observant parent will be alert both to small clues and to large patterns of behavior. By noticing these, a parent can often offer appropriate suggestions and experiences, and also learn whether the help and explanations already given have been adequate.

Children have their own styles of learning, every one unique. They also have their own timetables, according to which they are ready to do things, speeds at which they want

to do them, and time they want to wait before doing a new
thing. (p. 133)

Like all homeschooling parents, unschooling parents have the
time, and the insight that love and proximity provide, to recognize
the differences in their children. Being free from the constraints
of a specific structured curriculum, unschooling parents can adjust
the way they gently guide or direct each child according to his
specific learning style, temperament, etc. Much has been written
in recent years about learning styles, multiple intelligences, and so
on. The unschooling family is in a good position to take advantage
of such information, and help each child reach his unique potential. Holt shows that parents can take this delicate attentiveness
to a new level when they become aware of the varying needs of
one child.

> Adults have to be conscious of a rise and fall in children—like
> the rise and fall of the tide—of courage and confidence. Some
> days kids have a tiger in their tank. They're just raring to go;
> they're full of enthusiasm and confidence. If you knock them
> down, they bounce up. Other days, you scratch them and
> they pour out blood. What you can get them to try, and what
> you can get them to tolerate in the way of correction or ad-
> vice, depends enormously on how they feel, on how big their
> store of confidence and self-respect happens to be at the mo-
> ment. This may vary—it may vary even within the space of
> an hour.
>   If you don't punish a child when she isn't feeling brave,
> pretty soon she will feel brave. That is, if you don't outrun her
> store of courage, she will get braver. (pp. 155-156)

Let me reassure you that John Holt didn't expect all parents
to be perfect in their patience and sensitivity or in their ability to
restrain themselves from too much teaching. He did, however,
observe that these traits developed and grew as parents spent more
time with their children.

Can Unschooling Look Like School?

While these excerpts from Holt's books give us a clearer picture of what unschooling looks like, you may wonder if there is any resemblance between unschooling and traditional schooling or homeschooling. Can the unschooler ever use typically schoolish tools? In other words, can unschooling ever look like schooling?

The answer to this question will complete, for now, our sketch of unschooling. We find a thorough response to this concern in the recently published, new edition of *Teach Your Own*. Patrick Farenga, who was a friend and colleague of John Holt, and is now president of Holt Associates, revised the book. Since he and his wife Day are unschooling parents of three girls, Farenga was able to add the insights gained from his own experience as an unschooling father to John Holt's observations. In a chapter called "How to Get Started," Farenga describes unschooling and explains how it can sometimes resemble school. I will quote the passage at length so that it may touch up and highlight our picture of the unschooling family.

> The advantage of this method is that it doesn't require you, the parent, to become someone else, i.e., a professional teacher pouring knowledge into child-vessels on a planned basis. Instead you live and learn together, pursuing questions and interests as they arise and using conventional schooling on an "on-demand" basis, if at all. This is the way we learn before going to school and the way we learn when we leave school and enter the world of work. So, for instance, a young child's interest in hot rods can lead him to a study of how the engine works (science), how and when the car was built (history and business), who built and designed the car (biography), etc. Certainly these interests can lead to reading texts, taking courses, or doing projects, but the important difference is that these activities were chosen and engaged in freely by the learner. They were not dictated to the learner through curricular mandate to be done at a specific time and place, though

parents with a more hands-on approach to unschooling certainly can influence and guide their children's choices. Unschooling . . . is the natural way to learn. However, this does not mean unschoolers do not take traditional classes or use curricular materials when the student, or parents and children together, decide that this is how they want to do it. Learning to read or do quadratic equations are not "natural" processes, but unschoolers nonetheless learn them when it makes sense to them to do so, not because they have reached a certain age or are compelled to do so by arbitrary authority. Therefore it isn't unusual to find unschoolers who are barely eight years old studying astronomy or who are ten years old and just learning to read. (pp. 238-239)

We see, then, that unschooling can look like schooling. Unschoolers can use textbooks or take courses to learn, just like other children and adults do. However, as Pat Farenga points out, "These activities [are] chosen and engaged in freely by the learner." Unschooling families will cherish the freedom to pursue learning in innovative ways, and in traditional ways, depending on the circumstances. Trusting their children to learn, unschooling parents will provide them access to the world, and freedom to explore it. As John Holt has shown us, at their best unschooling families will look like loving, respectful people, who enjoy spending time living and learning together.

PART TWO:
CATHOLIC
UNSCHOOLING

CHAPTER FOUR:
CAN A CATHOLIC BE AN UNSCHOOLER?

You have now reached the heart of this book. My family's homeschooling journey, the definition and reasons for unschooling, and what unschooling looks like were all preliminaries building up to this central question: Can a Catholic, in good conscience, unschool? As I said at the outset, I am writing this book first for myself, and this question is the one I would most like to answer, once and for all.

In my own reading and thinking about homeschooling, the question of whether a Catholic can unschool continually returns to vex me. I frequently discuss it with my husband, whose reassuring explanations calm my anxiety and solve my difficulties. When I then peacefully consider Joseph's progress in knowledge, faith, and general growing up, I am pleased with the actual results of our unschooling approach. Because the unschooling movement grew out of secular roots, however, and because most unschoolers I have read about are not Christian, doubts do continue to arise. In addition, the enthusiasm with which Catholic homeschoolers promote the Montessori method, a classical curriculum, or traditional programs of schooling can awaken fears that unschooling is not only risky for Joseph, but an abdication of my parental duties.

My hope is that in writing about Catholic unschooling I can clarify and organize my thoughts and definitively vanquish my fears. At the least, I will have my own book to re-read when I am attacked by parenting scruples. In this chapter, I am going to expose my doubts to the light by writing about the two strongest objections to Catholic unschooling. I will then answer these objections in order to show that Catholics can responsibly choose unschooling for their families. Our consideration of whether Catholics can be unschoolers will thus hinge on overcoming Catholic objections to unschooling, rather than on making a case that unschooling is particularly Catholic. As I have already stated, I think there are many worthwhile options for Catholic education; I am concerned to show that unschooling is one such option, but not that it is the only one or even the very best one. In any specific family the parents' personalities and educational backgrounds, the children's learning styles and temperaments, the family's goals and priorities, will all contribute to determine which method of homeschooling works best for them. For us, unschooling has been most appealing and most effective; hence my desire to clear away Catholic objections to it.

The First Objection: Fallen Human Nature

A Catholic's strongest objection to unschooling is: how can this relaxed approach work, given fallen human nature? While we are natural learners, aren't we also lazy? Isn't it the case that we must take into account what we know about fallen man's weaknesses, and don't these prohibit us from taking unschooling seriously? In other words, how can a Catholic unschool, when unschooling seems to ignore man's fallen nature? In support of this objection, there is a papal statement to the effect that any educational theory must be based upon a true notion of man's nature, or it won't be trustworthy. In his 1929 encyclical *On the Christian Education of Youth*, Pope Pius XI wrote:

> Every method of education founded, wholly or in part, on the denial or forgetfulness of original sin and of grace, and relying on the sole powers of human nature, is unsound. Such, generally speaking, are those modern systems bearing various names which appeal to a pretended self-government and unrestrained freedom on the part of the child, and which diminish or even suppress the teacher's authority and action, attributing to the child an exclusive primacy of initiative, and an activity independent of any higher law, natural or divine, in the work of his education. (§60)

The Church's firm rejection of certain forms of education, as stated here by Pope Pius XI, would seem to prohibit the Catholic from unschooling. After all, the writers who promote and defend unschooling do often appeal to the child's autonomy and ability to direct himself. In our own descriptions of unschooling we have spoken of a diminished role for the teacher, and our definition specifically referred to the child as the primary agent of his education. The Catholic's suspicions of unschooling seem to be justified, for the Church seems to have clearly condemned it.

A closer reading of the Pope's words will lift this apparent condemnation, and show us that unschooling is not forbidden for Catholics. Note that the objectionable methods of education attribute to the child "an exclusive primacy of initiative . . . in the work of his education." We can respond that because the child is always the primary agent in his learning, it is fitting that he often be the initiator of his learning as well. This is precisely what unschooling allows. Unschooling, however, does not require that the child be the only or exclusive initiator. Moreover, the Pope is especially concerned with preventing parents and educators from withholding religious instruction on the false belief that the child must initiate every area of his formation and education. In our defense of unschooling we have emphasized the need for parents to refrain from over-teaching, and the importance of their actively respecting the child's ability to learn without too much interference. But this is not equivalent to saying that unschooling parents cannot initiate areas of study. Consequently, unschooling as we have defined it is not one of the modern systems of education the Pope here condemns.

Furthermore, reading on in this encyclical, we find in the next paragraph a description which more accurately applies to unschooling, and which the Pope then approves. Pope Pius XI states:

> If any of these terms are used, less properly, to denote the necessity of a gradually more active co-operation on the part of

the pupil in his own education, if the intention is to banish
from education despotism and violence, which, by the way,
just punishment is not, this would be correct, but in no way
new. It would mean only what has been taught and reduced
to practice by the Church in traditional Christian education,
in imitation of the method employed by God Himself towards
His creatures, of whom He demands active co-operation according to the nature of each; for His Wisdom "reacheth from
end to end mightily and ordereth all things sweetly." (§61)

I find this passage very reassuring. Here we see that the
Church not only allows for unschooling, but even places it in line
with her tradition. But might it be wishful thinking on my part to
see unschooling in this second paragraph rather than in the first
one we quoted? What if some unschoolers actually do claim "self-
government and unrestrained freedom on the part of the child"
and attribute to him "an activity independent of any higher law,
natural or divine, in the work of his education"?

John Holt is commonly recognized as the original and best
advocate of the modern unschooling movement. And it turns out
that he was very concerned with the idea of freedom, especially
freedom for children. One of his books, which I have not read,
promoted the rights of children to such an extent that it was highly
controversial, even in the permissive era of the 1970's. Given Holt's
ideas, is it inconsistent of me to identify unschooling with the second passage above, rather than with the first?

I don't think so. As I have explained, my family's
homeschooling has turned out to resemble what John Holt describes as unschooling. When I first read his books, I rejoiced to
find so much truth and beauty, and such good advice. As I have
read more of Holt's writings, I have been more impressed with his
wisdom. I do see it as a natural wisdom, however, which falls short
of the full truth of Revelation. And so, when I find myself in dis-
agreement with Holt's opinions, I simply set aside what I disagree
with, while still subscribing to much of what he says. It helps that
he tried to keep his conclusions about children and his suggestions

to parents closely tied to observation. Consequently, many of these conclusions and suggestions stand on their own, apart from his theories of freedom and children's rights. As Holt himself said in *How Children Learn*, "My aim in writing [this book] is not primarily to persuade educators and psychologists to swap new doctrines for old, but to persuade them to look at children, patiently, repeatedly, respectfully, and to hold off making theories and judgments about them until they have in their minds what most of them do not now have—a reasonably accurate model of what children are like" (p. 271).

Patrick Farenga succeeded John Holt as the publisher of *Growing Without Schooling* magazine, and is president of Holt Associates. Farenga has this to say: "When pressed, I define unschooling as allowing children as much freedom to learn in the world as their parents can comfortably bear" (*Teach Your Own*, p. 238). I take this to mean, among other things, that Catholic parents, who will set limits on the freedom they allow their children, can still consider themselves unschoolers.

What About Laziness?

Before we go on to the second objection, I want to be sure we have adequately answered the first. We have seen that Pope Pius XI's censure of certain methods of education does not apply to our understanding of unschooling. But the Catholic parent may still worry that unschooling does not take into account the results of the fall. He may frame his objection thus: Due to the fall, we all suffer from laziness. If we are not made to do things, we take the path of least resistance and do nothing. Children, especially, must be made to learn and do assigned schoolwork, otherwise they will do nothing, or at least nothing they find difficult, and will fail to learn what they need to know. Unschooling wrongly attributes to children powers of initiative and an ability to follow through that they don't have; therefore, unschooling won't work.

I think that this version of the fallen human nature objection is very persuasive. Nonetheless, I think it contains so many errors that I don't know just where to begin! Six important points come to mind.

First, the Catholic may have in mind the capital sin of sloth. This sin is often misunderstood as laziness, when it actually has a different meaning. Sloth, also called *acedia*, is not a sin against industriousness, but a sin against charity. The *Catechism of the Catholic Church* teaches: "One can sin against God's love in various ways: . . . *acedia* or spiritual sloth goes so far as to refuse the joy that comes from God and to be repelled by divine goodness" (§2094). And also, "Another temptation [in prayer], to which presumption opens the gate, is *acedia*. The spiritual writers understand by this a form of depression due to lax ascetical practice, decreased vigilance, carelessness of heart. 'The spirit indeed is willing, but the flesh is weak' (Mt 26:41)" (§2733). What we think of as the capital sin of laziness is really the capital sin of sloth, or *acedia*. It is not a sin against industriousness, but a sin against the love of God.

Second, to the extent that laziness is an imperfection, venial sin, or weakness resulting from the fall, its remedy will be grace, not hard work. As Catholics, we do not profess that "God only helps those who help themselves," nor that we must whip ourselves and our children into top shape. Instead, "In vain is your earlier rising, your going later to rest, you who toil for the bread you eat: when He pours gifts on His beloved while they slumber" (Psalm 126). I take this to mean that our Heavenly Father is not waiting for us to pull ourselves up by our bootstraps, nor is He too concerned with our efficiency. Rather, He delights in pouring out His grace upon us; all we need to do is let Him. We can give our children access to the world of grace by introducing them to the sacraments and the practice of prayer. These will help them to overcome the results of the fall in their own lives.

Third, we must constantly remind ourselves that, as Mother

Teresa said, "We are not called to be successful, but only to be faithful." Perhaps this is why the Church identifies *acedia*, not laziness, as a capital sin. As Catholic parents we will want to teach our children that loving God and doing His will are our first priorities, rather than worldly ambition, or a drive to succeed, even in academic realms.

Fourth, let's take a closer look at the complaint that if we are not made to do anything, we will do nothing. John Holt addresses this point with dispatch; he says that this is the creed of a slave. The following passage from *How Children Fail* deserves our serious reflection. Holt writes:

> So many people have said to me, "If we didn't make children do things, they wouldn't do anything." Even worse, they say, "If I weren't made to do things, I wouldn't do anything."

> It is the creed of a slave.

> When people say that terrible thing about themselves, I say, "You may believe that, but I don't believe it. You didn't feel that way about yourself when you were little. Who taught you to feel that way?" To a large degree, it was school. Do the schools teach this message by accident, or on purpose? I don't know, and I don't think they know. They teach it because, believing it, they can't help acting as if it were true. (p. 113)

Fifth, we need to realize that although John Holt did not, as far as we can tell, believe in the doctrine of fallen human nature, the children he observed were certainly still subject to it. His experience was that children are eager learners, and his conviction was strengthened by the homeschoolers who wrote to *Growing Without Schooling*. For over twenty years the magazine's pages were full of personal accounts of unschooled children, their interests, pursuits, and achievements. It is fascinating and inspiring reading, sure to convince the skeptic that Holt was right: children are natural learners. They want to do what grown-ups do, they want to make sense of things, and given some access to the world, they will work hard to understand it. My point here is that all these children suffered the effects of fallen human nature, even if they, their parents, or John Holt didn't know it. Yet they consistently pursued their interests and knowledge of the world around them. From this I conclude that while our nature has been damaged by the fall, we are not so devastated that we cease striving to learn.

Sixth, how much more will our children strive and learn when we can assist them with the graces of the sacraments and prayer? As I mentioned above, these are the remedies that heal and strengthen our wounded nature. When we see the beautiful achievements and maturity of unschooled children who don't have the benefits of our religion, we can only imagine that with the assistance of our Mother, the Church, our children will love and enjoy life and learning in ways we will have to see to believe.

Let that suffice for our response to the question of how unschooling can work given fallen human nature. We saw that Pope Pius XI did not condemn unschooling in *On the Christian Education of Youth*; rather, he seemed to acknowledge certain aspects of unschooling as being in accord with the traditional teaching of the Church. Moreover, we showed that the Catholic's fear of laziness as an impediment to unschooling was also unfounded. We must now consider the other main objection a Catholic is likely to raise against unschooling.

The Second Objection: Our Duty to Teach the Faith

Simply put, as Catholic parents we will have a fourth "R" to teach our children; along with reading, writing, and 'rithmetic, we will want our kids to learn religion. While we may trust them to pick up the first three of these on their own, we cannot leave their knowledge of the Catholic faith to chance. Our goal as parents is to raise our kids to be saints, to get them to Heaven. Hence our chief duty is to pass on to them the Catholic faith, and this will require us to teach them the revealed doctrines we believe and why we believe them. Since unschooling means letting children discover by themselves what they need to know, we Catholics cannot be unschoolers.

This objection is important because it brings to the fore our end in the education of our children. Catholic education is for the children's sake because its goal is the happiness of children both in this life and, most importantly, in the life to come. We believe that the life of grace is an anticipation of Heaven, so our heavenly happiness begins now on this earth. This earthly happiness of incomplete knowledge and love of God is meant to be crowned with the perfect happiness of Heaven, when our knowledge and love of God are completed by our transforming union with Him.

In our definition of unschooling we stated that we trust the child to learn what he needs to know to lead him to happiness. For the Catholic this would mean trusting the child to learn what he needs to know to lead him to Heaven, his ultimate happiness. Isn't this too much to expect a child to discover on his own?

We can respond that yes, it is too much to expect a child to discover on his own. Our understanding of unschooling, however, does not require us to leave the child to discover everything by himself. Remember that we called the parents the secondary agents in the child's education, because they will guide and oversee his learning. This guidance can include helping him to learn things, and providing him with the best possible materials to help him learn. In other words, the Catholic unschooling parent does not have to (and in fact, will not) leave his children to discover the Faith "on their own." As we said at the end of the last chapter, unschoolers can even use traditional schoolish means such as textbooks (or in this case, catechisms) without compromising their status as unschoolers.

Rather than presenting a difficulty, this objection illuminates for us the picture of the Catholic unschooling family. The parents provide a rich Catholic environment for the children, with holy pictures, sacramentals, and many wonderful Catholic books filling the home. Some of these the parents acquire in order to nurture the Faith in their children, but because they themselves love these things, the atmosphere will not be stilted or artificial. The children see that their parents love and live the Faith, and wanting to be like their parents, they too will begin to love and live the Faith. Their parents are in love with Jesus, and get to receive Him in Holy Communion. The children want to do that too! They want to love Jesus, to be His friends, to have Him come to them in this special way. These children have been baptized as infants, and the supernatural virtues of faith, hope and charity are seeds waiting to grow. The parents will nurture these seeds through their example, their Catholic home life, and the many conversations they have with the children. The "teaching" of the Catholic faith will happen so naturally, that the parents will find themselves edified by their children's insights and love. As John Holt said, "It is love, not tricks and techniques of thought, that lies at the heart of all true learning." This applies especially to learning our religion, which is itself entirely about love.

In fact, there is a close affinity between unschooling, which sees life and learning and love inextricably entwined, and Catholic catechesis in the home. Pope John Paul II wrote in *Catechesi Tradendae* (his letter on *Catechesis in Our Time*):

> Education in the faith by parents, which should begin from the children's tenderest age, is already being given when the members of a family help each other to grow in faith through the witness of their Christian lives, a witness that is often without words but which perseveres throughout a day-to-day life lived in accordance with the Gospel. This catechesis is more incisive when, in the course of family events (such as the reception of the sacraments, the celebration of great liturgical feasts, the birth of a child, a bereavement) care is taken to explain in the home the Christian or religious content of these events. But that is not enough: Christian parents must strive to follow and repeat, within the setting of family life, the more

methodical teaching received elsewhere. The fact that these truths about the main questions of faith and Christian living are thus repeated within a family setting impregnated with love and respect will often make it possible to influence the children in a decisive way for life. The parents themselves profit from the effort that this demands of them, for in a catechetical dialogue of this sort each individual both receives and gives. (§68)

In other words, the education in the Faith that parents need to provide is not just bookish knowledge. To effectively catechize their children, parents must live the Faith with them. This will include conversations and explanations, but equally important will be "a witness that is often without words." Far from being an impediment to unschooling, our duty to pass on the Faith to our children will become the richest part of Catholic unschooling.

We see, then, that the two strongest Catholic objections to unschooling do not hold up. We will have to contend with our fallen human nature until we are perfectly healed in Heaven, but it does not prevent us from learning, and is not an insuperable obstacle to unschooling. As Catholic parents, we have a grave responsibility to educate our children in the Faith. But again, this does not present any problem for unschooling. Unschooling does not prevent our passing on the Faith to our children; instead, it can help to provide the kind of environment that the Holy Father recommends.

In the end, these objections fail to prove that a Catholic cannot be an unschooler. Despite my anxiety, and in accord with my husband's repeated assurances, we have reason to think that Catholics can unschool their children with confidence. In the next chapter we will consider what Catholic unschooling might look like. We have shown that Catholics can unschool with a clean conscience. Let us now try to calm any residual fears by looking at some Catholics who do unschool.

CHAPTER FIVE:
WHAT CATHOLIC UNSCHOOLING
LOOKS LIKE

Like a shepherd He feeds His flock; in His
arms He gathers the lambs, carrying them in
His bosom, and leading the ewes with care.
(Isaiah 40:11)

In our description of what unschooling looks like, we veered away from giving examples of particular unschooling families. Instead we stuck to a more general outline, since differing circumstances will determine the specific details of each family's unschooling life. When we now consider what Catholic unschooling looks like, the same holds true: namely, that varying circumstances will lead different Catholic families to pursue their learning adventures in diverse ways. It is also true, however, that a picture is worth a thousand words, and so I offer here a picture (albeit in words) of one Catholic unschooling family in order to complement the previous more general description of what unschooling looks like. I also hope that this picture will help potential Catholic unschoolers begin to imagine how they might proceed.

First a couple of preliminary remarks. I think it is worth repeating with Patrick Farenga that unschooling can sometimes employ elements, such as textbooks, that make it look like traditional schooling. For Catholic unschoolers, such a resemblance would arise if, for example, a family chose to learn Catholic doctrine by studying the *Baltimore Catechism*. Such an approach might supplement the family's devotional life and provide a starting point for discussions about their Catholic beliefs and practices. As we explained, every aid to learning, whether "schoolish" or "innovative," is a possible resource for the unschooler.

49

Also keep in mind that unschooling does not by definition exclude discipline and structure. Neither does it exclude goal-setting. In other words, Catholic unschooling parents may look a lot like other Catholic homeschooling parents as they plan what each of their children needs to do to contribute to the common good of the family (such as individual chores), and how their day will be ordered (perhaps Mass together in the morning, meals at set times, etc.). They will also likely resemble other parents as they discuss each child's special interests, talents, and spiritual and intellectual development. Catholic unschoolers might look different from other homeschoolers when they map out strategies for helping the children achieve their goals; by definition there will be more input from the children about their course of studies/pursuits, and the plans will probably be quite individualized for each child.

These things said, let us turn to see what one real Catholic unschooling family looks like. I hope you will not be too surprised or disappointed when I tell you that the family you will see is my own! After all, I can describe fairly accurately what goes on around our house, and I won't need to change the names to protect our identities. I can also check with Tony and Joseph to assure that there is some likeness between my description and the family I'm trying to capture. Since I have already told you about our journey to unschooling, in this chapter I will focus on what our unschooling has looked like recently.

Our Version of Catholic Unschooling

For the last couple of years, Joseph has been involved with ongoing activities outside our home. He is a member of the Junior Legion of Mary, is an altar boy in our parish, and attends our family holy hour once a week. This year he had his first experience with organized team sports, playing basketball on our parish's church-league team with his cousin Vince and other friends. We belong to a Catholic sports and social club, and there Joseph has attended six-week P.E. mini-courses with other homeschooled kids his age. As for formal lessons, he has been taking piano from a wonderful local teacher for three years now. He has lessons once a week, with theory written work and daily practice expected between lessons, and group recitals twice a year. While he does a fairly good job estimating just how little work he can get away with, I allow myself to be his conscience about actually getting to the piano each day. (Isn't "conscience" a nicer word than "nag"?)

Within the home, Joseph's daily schedule includes taking care of his overgrown terrier Toby, helping me with baby Dominic, and reading from morning until night. He works sporadically on math textbooks or workbook pages during the official school year, and this year we actually conquered fractions and decimals. Well, Joseph did. My math skills are a bit rusty and I am grateful that he likes to work on his own.

Any interstices between these activities in and out of the home Joseph fills with play, reading, and more play. My sister-in-law's homeschooling family lives down the street, and Joseph is delighted to spend some time with his eight cousins almost every day. He and age-mate Vince play action figures, basketball, Star Wars trading cards, Lego's, and more.

For our religious education, over the years we have used the *Baltimore Catechism*, Ignatius Press' *Faith and Life* series, materials from Seton Home Study School, and books on the Saints' lives. Each of these had something to offer us at the right time, but the last two years we found a new approach. For our Catholic doctrine, I read to Joseph from Monsignor Ronald Knox's *The Creed in Slow Motion*. This book is a series of sermons given to schoolgirls in England during World War II. We would read one chapter at a sitting, each chapter being a single sermon on an article of the Apostle's Creed. Somehow we managed to stretch the book out over two years (sixth and seventh grades), and I almost feel ready to start it again for eighth! Knox had a great sense of humor that kept Joseph and I smiling, and an engaging style that we thoroughly enjoyed. We both learned a lot, and laughed a lot too.

We have tried to make reading aloud a central feature of our unschooling, although too often it gets pushed aside in the bustle of daily life. From his earliest years, Joseph has been surrounded by books, and over time he would sit for longer periods to listen while we read to him. This was an easy way for me to entertain him, since reading is my favorite activity. Eventually we got Dad more involved, and he read to us two of our all-time best stories: to both of us, he read *Leave it to Psmith* by P. G. Wodehouse (a sure antidote to Lenten blues), and to Joseph he read the complete *Lord of the Rings* (over the course of a summer). Sometimes in our desire to keep a particular session going, Tony and I will switch off reading aloud, chapter by chapter, or as our voices weaken. I should mention that because Joseph has always hated and resisted reading out loud himself (though he loves to listen), I have never made him do so. This hasn't affected his love of reading to himself, and he does sometimes read aloud to me a particularly funny passage from whatever book he's currently enjoying.

Because I am a book lover constantly on the lookout for good books to add to our collection, Joseph has a large library at his disposal right downstairs. Through his reading he has become quite familiar with history, geography, and literature. This year he has enjoyed going through our vast supply of P. G. Wodehouse novels, and the fiction of G. K. Chesterton. It is heart-warming to me to see him still dipping into our "kid's books" too, re-reading old favorites and gamely checking out any new arrivals.

I think that our particular style of unschooling has worked so well for us because Joseph loves to read. Books have opened up for him the areas of Church history, natural science, mythology, fantasy, and more. His learning in these "subject areas" has been painless and seemingly effortless.

Joseph's knowledge of history and geography is, in fact, an excellent instance of our unschooling at its best. He loves to read everything, from Landmark children's books to historical atlases to illustrated gun, uniform, and flag books. (Oh yes, and comic books,

Lego Mania magazines, and cereal boxes too!) For years I brought Saints' biographies to Sunday Mass with us, so that he could read during the sermons. He didn't seem ready to understand the homilies, and I wasn't ready to explain certain sins that our holy priests preached against. All of this reading has fostered his interest in and understanding of history and geography. I confess here, for the record, that my role was as book provider, but I could not give positive knowledge, for I don't have it to give in these areas.

I was impishly amused when my father once praised me for imparting my knowledge of history and geography to Joseph; he thought I had taught these to my son. Tony, who like Joseph has learned lots of history through a lifetime of reading encyclopedias at the breakfast table, can vouch for my continued ignorance compounded by error in these fields. I did manage to commit to memory a few basic facts about the Civil War when we moved to Virginia. It was getting embarrassing not to know which side was the blue and which was the gray, that Stonewall Jackson and Robert E. Lee were on the Southern, also called Confederate side, and that General U. S. Grant was on the Northern, or Union, team. There you have almost all of my knowledge of military history in one place. I hope I got it right!

Since I am revealing family secrets, I might as well confess another key to our unschooling. Joseph has never enjoyed learning from me when I attempted to teach him new concepts. We have had some of our best times together when I read aloud, when we had special late-night feasts and conversations, and when we went on adventures to new places nearby. We really love each other's company, and baby Dominic has made life together even more of a treat. But our schooling has definitely improved as I began to follow John Holt's advice and hold back on the teaching, in order to let Joseph learn. I recognized myself in Holt's critique of teachers who try to force knowledge into children. How many times Joseph and I ended up in tears of anger when I tried to teach him something, despite his resistance.

Such resistance in children can have many causes, such as lack of readiness, fear of failure, tiredness . . . and with Joseph I'm sure there were different causes on various occasions. Unfortunately, most of the times that we reached an impasse over a math lesson or the like, I would be blinded by frustration and insist on continuing the lesson, despite Joseph's unwillingness. I often misinterpreted his genuine confusion, and thought he was being obstinate. This led to my vain attempts to win the apparent battle of the wills. In our case, always a mistake! It was a great help to read John Holt and realize that I needed to relax. While Joseph resisted my teaching, he did not resist learning. No, he was learning all the time. His knowledge in the areas of my ignorance proves to me that he did learn without my teaching. And for those new math concepts, I have tried to supply clear, self-teaching materials that Joseph can use on his own.

As we go along, Joseph and I have interesting conversations about what we are doing. Our school year mimics that of my husband, since he is a college professor and has a set schedule for his classes from late August to early May. At the end of our Christmas break this last year, I half-jokingly spoke to Joseph of our "last day of freedom." He heartily agreed and moaned about starting up again. I reminded him that what we did for his education was pretty easy, consisting daily of a couple of math pages, his piano assignments, and listening to Monsignor Knox for religion. He replied, "I realize that it's minimal, practically nominal work, but it is still work!" Then when I said I had read a lot about unschooling, but wasn't ready to give up all formal assignments (i.e. math pages), he responded, "Oh no, I do want to know the basics of math!"

To me this episode highlights the joy of unschooling. For our family unschooling includes a school-year calendar and some formal math, but these are undertaken in a spirit of cooperation. When, being the pitiful creatures we are, we complain about the work we've chosen, it is good to reflect that in our better moments we decided upon the work together.

Because it is hard to let go of the feeling that school is work (for us as unschoolers, it is "minimal, practically nominal work, but still work"), I like to take the summers "off." Of course, the learning is happening all year round, but in my experience it is a constant challenge to trust, to remember that unschooling makes sense, to relax. Summer is a time when we can do nothing schoolish, and not feel guilty about what we're not doing! One of my goals is to overcome needless guilt during the school year too, but that is a matter of learning to trust, and takes time.

CHAPTER SIX:
SHOULD ALL CATHOLICS UNSCHOOL?

The only happiness here below is to strive to
be always content with what Jesus gives us.
-St. Thérèse of Lisieux

Having written the previous pages in defense of Catholic
unschooling, I add this chapter lest I be misunderstood. I am not
advocating unschooling as the best homeschooling style for every
family. In fact, I have argued that unschooling can work, and that
it is an option for Catholic homeschoolers. I want, however, to
follow the Church in all things, and it seems to me that the Church
as the perfect Mother and Teacher carefully guards the uniqueness
of her children, as well as providing for their common needs. I do
not want to be more narrow than the Church, and the Church
allows for many different forms of education.

While God has made all of us out of love, that we may be
united with Him in love, He has expressed the immensity of His
perfection by creating each of us as unique individuals. Fr. Pichon,
a holy Jesuit and spiritual director of St. Thérèse's family, said that
there is more variation between souls than between faces. Therefore it should not surprise us that the Church allows and encour-
ages her children to follow a variety of paths up the mountain that
is Christ. We see this beautifully incarnated in the variety of religious orders and their charisms.

As Jesus said the night before He died, "Let not your heart be
troubled . . . . In my Father's house there are many mansions.
Were it not so, I should have told you, because I go to prepare a
place for you" (Jn 14:1-2). Reflecting on our own experience, we
can see that not all Catholic homeschoolers need to unschool.
Along with the proverbial, "Success is not where it's at," I also like
the saying, "Don't mess with success." On the one hand, let us

avoid putting pressure on ourselves to achieve great things. On the other hand, when we find the method that works for us, we should embrace the blessings which flow from living in the way that suits our family.

If you have already discovered a style that works well for you and your children, I encourage you to continue as you are. By writing this book, I mean to present one effective way to learn at home. I hope to encourage the fainthearted who would like to try unschooling; I do not mean to propose unschooling as the only or best Catholic way.

As Catholic homeschooling has grown, more educational approaches have been tried and proved helpful in the home. Consider the following examples: Mary Kay Clark wrote *Catholic Homeschooling* and runs the popular Seton Home Study School. Laura Berquist has written the book *How to Design Your Own Classical Curriculum*, and now provides classical curricula syllabi through Our Lady of Divine Grace School. Kimberly Hahn and Mary Hasson co-authored *Catholic Education: Homeward Bound* while Rachel Mackson and Maureen Wittman edited *A Catholic Homeschool Treasury*. Both of these books contain a wealth of information about many homeschooling approaches which the authors, and other Catholic parents, have found effective. Most recently, Elizabeth Foss has published *Real Learning: Education in the Heart of the Home*, in which she presents a Catholic guide to Charlotte Mason-style home learning. And finally, many Catholic mothers have enjoyed integrating a Montessori approach into their homeschools. All of these approaches have their champions and their satisfied customers. We can only admire and praise God for the breadth of opportunities available to us in this new springtime of the Church.

St. Thérèse has said at the beginning of her memoir *Story of A Soul* what I am trying to say here.

> Jesus deigned to teach me this mystery. He set before me the
> book of nature; I understood how all the flowers He has cre-

ated are beautiful, how the splendor of the rose and the white-ness of the Lily do not take away the perfume of the little vio-let or the delightful simplicity of the daisy. I understood that if all flowers wanted to be roses, nature would lose her spring-time beauty, and the fields would no longer be decked out with little wild flowers.

And so it is in the world of souls, Jesus' garden. He willed to create great souls comparable to Lilies and roses, but He has created smaller ones and these must be content to be dai-sies or violets destined to give joy to God's glances when He looks down at His feet. Perfection consists in doing His will, in being what He wills us to be.

I understood, too, that Our Lord's love is revealed as per-fectly in the most simple soul who resists His grace in nothing as in the most excellent soul; in fact, since the nature of love is to humble oneself, if all souls resembled those of the holy Doc-tors who illumined the Church with the clarity of their teach-ings, it seems God would not descend so low when coming to their heart. But He created the child who knows only how to make his feeble cry heard; He has created the poor savage who has nothing but the natural law to guide him. It is to their hearts that God deigns to lower Himself. These are the wild flowers whose simplicity attracts Him. When coming down in this way, God manifests His infinite grandeur. Just as the sun shines simultaneously on the tall cedars and on each little flower as though it were alone on the earth, so Our Lord is occupied particularly with each soul as though there were no others like it. And just as in nature all the seasons are ar-ranged in such a way as to make the humblest daisy bloom on a set day, in the same way, everything works out for the good of each soul.

It has taken years of trial and error, along with the grace of God, for us to find the homeschooling approach that fits our family best. I have enjoyed writing about our experience in the hope of helping other families to discern how God is leading them. Whether you choose to unschool, to stick with another method of homeschooling, or even to send your kids to school, the important thing is to do God's will. As parents working hard to lead our children toward Heaven, we need to remember the words of St. Thérèse: "Perfection [for us and our children] consists in doing His will, in being what He wills us to be . . . . And just as in nature all the seasons are arranged in such a way as to make the humblest daisy bloom on a set day, in the same way, everything works out for the good of each soul."

In the remaining chapters of this book, I want to offer you encouragement in whatever path God wills you to take. It is my experience that mothers, especially, have to constantly battle anxiety as they oversee their children's education. Anything we can do to encourage one another and lighten that load is of primary importance, for Christ wants us to have peace. I have found three ways to keep my spirits up as I unschool my children, and each seems as necessary as the others. Trusting nature, trusting God, and finding comfort in books: these are my helps along the way. I gladly share them with you in the following pages.

PART THREE:

HELPS ALONG THE WAY

CHAPTER SEVEN:
LEARNING TO TRUST NATURE

As I write this book, my eight-month-old son Dominic is beginning to eat solid food. He has been a good little nurser, and those who meet him are impressed with his robust physique. But he has been resisting the introduction of solids, rejecting them with a combination of funny faces and a strong gag reflex. Just last night, however, I watched in awe as he accepted a baby spoonful of Gerber pears. He tasted, didn't grimace, and swallowed.

"He's eating!" I announced with astonishment. As relief washed over me, I realized I had been afraid that he'd never learn to eat. Suddenly it came over me in a flash, the mother's refrain: "What if he never learns to eat? What if he never gets potty-trained? What if he never learns to read?" I burst out laughing. I was thinking how funny it is that we worry over things which will come so naturally when the time is right.

"You know," I said to Tony, "We don't trust nature at all."

"Of course we don't," he responded. "Nature comes from God, and we don't trust God."

If you are anything like me, you may be convinced that unschooling is reasonable; you may even desire to start unschooling with your family, but there is still a lingering doubt. Sure, it looks good on paper, but what if my kids don't have any interests, or never learn to read? The list goes on and on.

Another recent conversation in our home will illustrate the imaginative form such fears can assume. The other night, I decided it was time to admit my latest anxiety to my husband. "Tony," I said, "I know this is silly, but lately I've been worrying. What if Dominic never learns to read? What if he never even learns what books are for?" I was thinking about how he only wants to teethe on his board books, and I was feeling guilty that I have not tried to read them to him yet. Tony could not restrain himself from a candid, if insensitive, response: "Don't worry, he can't possibly not know what books are for as long as you're still alive!" I had to laugh, as I realized how silly my fears were. It is true, a mother can manage to worry and feel guilty about anything, no matter how ridiculous.

Will They Learn?

We also find ourselves all too often allowing our groundless fears to determine the way we relate to our children. I find it encouraging to know I am not alone in my tendency to distrust my children, despite all my attempts to remember they are natural learners. I love the following story told by Nancy Wallace, a friend of John Holt. Holt often visited Nancy, her husband Bob, their son Ishmael and daughter Vita. About one such visit, Nancy writes:

> One afternoon, while John was snoozing on the couch, Vita and I decided to do a little math. (No, I still hadn't learned my lesson!) We had just started learning how to divide fractions and as luck would have it, Vita asked me why it was, anyway, that when all you were really trying to do was divide fractions, you not only had to take the second fraction and turn it upside-down, but then you had to multiply and not divide, which was what you were supposed to be doing in the first place. The textbook that we were using had some sort of confusing explanation that made us both more confused than ever, and finally, since Vita was tired anyway, she burst into tears. (A homeschooler's nightmare, I couldn't help thinking—to make your kid cry over a math problem right in front of John Holt!)
>
> John could never bear to hear children cry, and his eyes popped open with Vita's first sobs. "What's the trouble, Lambkin?" he asked. She was in no mood to answer and so I said, "Oh, it's nothing really. We shouldn't have tried to divide fractions when she was too tired." "Maybe I can help," he said. "Let me look at the book." Well, I couldn't help thinking that now we were in for real trouble. Vita was red in the face and she looked as if she wasn't about to let anybody try to tell

her anything. Dutifully, though, she gave John the book, and sat down next to him. He looked over it and then spent some time just staring off into space while Vita looked at him curiously. Then he began talking to himself and scribbling on a piece of paper. Vita watched, and listened, and gradually John began directing his talk to her, almost as if she was just an extension of himself. And she, meanwhile, was becoming totally involved in what he was doing, which was trying to work out a simple proof to answer her question. By the time he had actually worked it out, Vita was right with him, and I think they were both equally thrilled. "Pleased as punch," as he used to say. (*Child's Work*, pp. 93-94)

I first read this story a year ago, in an issue of *Growing Without Schooling* that paid tribute to John Holt after his death in 1985. I came across it again in Nancy's book *Child's Work*. In this book, as well as in her first book *Better Than School*, she discusses the difficulty of learning to trust her children to learn. She had to work hard to control her own fears, and allow them the freedom to pursue their interests. Her second book was published in 1990, when her children were still learning at home. Upon reading it in 2003, I had to know how Ishmael and Vita had "turned out." A little research on the internet and I discovered that Ishmael is now a professional pianist and composer of operas, chamber music, and orchestral works. Vita is a professional violinist, and together they have performed around the world as the Orfeo Duo. It seems that, as in childhood, they remain best friends.

Alison McKee is another mother who has written about her struggle to trust her children's ability to learn. In *Homeschooling Our Children, Unschooling Ourselves*, she tells us that her mantra was "Show me the way; show me the way." She repeated this silently, constantly reminding herself to look to the children to show her their best ways to learn. When I ordered the book from her, Alison sent with it a personal letter updating me on her children's latest endeavors. She must have known I have an enquiring mind! Her son graduated from college with honors, and went on to do a year of volunteer work in inner city schools. Among other interesting plans, he was thinking of attending law school in the future. Her daughter, at the time Alison wrote to me, was studying acting and attending college, as well as working on becoming a sign language interpreter. She loves Shakespeare, enjoys singing, and plans eventually to get her Master's Degree. Alison wrote, "Who would have thought unschooling would be such a success?"

It is a comfort to discover that we are not the only ones struggling to trust, and to hear stories of unschooled children who actually did learn and grow into happy, productive adults. Nonetheless, on a day-to-day basis we still find ourselves living with our own children and wondering nervously: What if they are the exception to nature's rule? With this recurrent anxiety, of course we also wonder how in the world we can find the courage to unschool. As we have seen, unschooling requires us to trust our children to learn. It is a daily struggle for me to trust that someday Joseph will learn the importance of brushing his teeth . . . how can I possibly trust that he'll learn everything else he needs to know?

Battles over personal grooming aside, we must admit that we do have good reasons to trust that our children will learn. In this book we have reviewed some of these reasons. I also recommend reading whatever you can about unschooling families and their children's learning experiences. The breadth and depth of such children's interests and knowledge is extremely encouraging. Then watch your own children, talk to them, read a good book to them, and you will be reminded that they are amazing people. Nature is at work in them, and they do delight in their senses; they do desire to know, and they do learn.

But Will They Learn Enough?

Even with these supports, however, our emotions often get the best of us, and we forget what we've seen and what we know. When we realize that our children have learned, are learning, and will continue to learn, the anxious doubt rephrases itself: Will they learn enough? Will they leave the nest knowing all they need to know? Will there be gaps in their education? I remember a funny conversation I had when we were beginning to homeschool Joseph. Although we were only doing first grade, I immediately started to panic about whether he would get into college! Since my husband is a college philosophy professor, I had easy access to a college admissions director, who also happens to be a homeschooling father. Running into Paul after Mass one morning, I asked him, "What do I need to teach Joseph so he will be ready for college when the time comes?" Paul smiled and explained, "You don't have to worry about the particulars. Just try to instill in him a love for learning, and he'll be all set." I walked away disappointed. "Of course we want him to love learning," I thought. "But what about the particulars? What exactly does he need to know?"

Seven years later, I frequently recall this conversation with a smile of my own. I see now that the modern compulsory school system has skewed our vision. Its proliferation of scope and sequence charts, the new standards of learning, and outcome-based education have all affected our expectations and perceptions of both education and learning. We imagine that learning = education = schooling, and that we have twelve years (not counting kindergarten and preschool) in which to pour all necessary information into the little brains under our care. We want to know precisely what to teach, and if we become enamored of unschooling, we want to know precisely what the children need to learn. "Yes, they are natural learners. I don't have to teach them everything; I can facilitate their learning," we muse. And then we ask, "But how can I be sure they will learn everything?"

Consider that last question. "How can I be sure they will learn everything?" Sometimes we narrow it to "How can I be sure they will learn everything they need to know?" This can be further specified according to our plans for each child: "How can I be sure Joseph will learn everything he needs to know to go to a good

Catholic college?" Yet as Paul implied years ago, there is not a list of subjects or facts that comprises the perfect education. I periodically remind myself that I have retained very little of what I learned in grade school and high school. Furthermore I continue to delve into new areas of study that awaken wonder and enrich my life. In my mid-thirties I became fascinated with birds, and have shared this newfound enthusiasm with family and friends. Having spent most of my life knowing almost nothing about the natural world, I now enjoy filling in the gaps (craters, actually) left yawning after twenty-three years of formal education. But far from being painful, this filling in is such fun!

Not only will you have fun, but as you begin to love learning together, you will be surprised at the world's reaction to your children. About once a month Joseph and I used to treat ourselves to a nearby Chinese buffet lunch. We became favorites of the manager because we always brought books and read while we ate. Joseph was plied with shirley-temples and called "scholar-boy," petted and praised by this kind Taiwanese man. We told him that we homeschooled, and he responded, "You keep reading. You skala-boy. You become fine smart man." We were a bit embarrassed over the attention, but appreciated his sincere encouragement. He told us about his advanced degrees from Spain, and that his children were college students. His repeated advice was, "Keep reading!" Our friendship with this man helped convince me that our children will be impressive to others even though that is not our goal.

The world needs interesting and interested citizens, not prodigies. We do not need to pass on to our children a large body of information before they leave us. Instead, we need to support our children in their natural learning and the development of their special gifts. Finally, we need to change our outlook. Instead of focusing on giving our children a complete education, or a perfect education (neither of which are necessary or possible), let us strive to awaken in them a love of learning. If we can help them to develop an attitude of life-long learning, we will have done enough. This fresh perspective will enable us to relax and enjoy the time we have to learn with our children, easing the pressure to hurry up and teach them "everything." As a friend of mine once said, on learning that I hadn't read any of Elizabeth Goudge's novels, "I envy you! You have so much to look forward to!" Instead of fearing that our children will have more to learn when they leave home, let us rejoice that none of us will ever be finished learning. We do indeed have so much to look forward to.

CHAPTER EIGHT:
LEARNING TO TRUST GOD

> If the Lord does not build the house,
> In vain do its builders labor;
> If the Lord does not watch over the city,
> In vain does the watchman keep vigil.
> In vain is your earlier rising,
> Your going later to rest,
> You who toil for the bread you eat:
> When He pours gifts on His beloved while they slumber.
>
> (from Psalm 127)

The purpose of this book has been to assuage fear and instill trust, by presenting the reasons for Catholic unschooling. By thinking through and articulating the rationale for the homeschooling approach that works for us, I hope to gain confidence in myself, my children, and our unschooling ways. I know, however, that doubts will continue to arise, for there is a limit to my ability to reassure myself; there is even a limit to my husband's ability to reassure me. The problem gets back to what he said about our lack of trust. "Of course we don't trust nature. Nature comes from God, and we don't trust God." So far I have outlined ways we can learn to trust nature. But to trust nature more completely, and conquer our fears more effectively, we must learn to trust God, the Author of nature.

To learn to trust Him, we need to spend time getting to know Him. What we need more than anything is to follow His advice. "Be still," He said, "and know that I am God" (Ps 46:10). St. John of the Cross puts it this way in his *Sayings of Light and Love*:

> If you desire to discover peace and consolation for your soul and to serve God truly, do not find your satisfaction in what you have left behind, because in that which now concerns you you may be as impeded as you were before, or even more. But leave as well all these other things and attend to one thing

alone that brings all these with it (namely, holy solitude, together with prayer and spiritual and divine reading), and persevere there in forgetfulness of all things. For if these things are not incumbent on you, you will be more pleasing to God in knowing how to guard and perfect yourself than by gaining all other things together; *what profit would there be for one to gain the whole world and suffer the loss of one's soul?* (§79)

Spending Time with God in Prayer

While the Catholic homeschooling mother may not have much time to herself to "persevere there in forgetfulness of all things," still any amount of time she can carve out of her day for prayer will be time well spent, and God will honor her little efforts. Certainly, as St. Teresa of Jesus said, we can find God among the pots and pans. But if we can also spend some time alone with the Alone, our many responsibilities will fall into their proper perspective. How many times are we anxious and concerned over many things, when truly only one thing is necessary?

I do not want to discount the difficulties we run up against when we, as mothers, try to steal away for a few minutes alone with Jesus. But I do think that He knows what we need, and that is time with Him. He wouldn't ask the impossible, so there must be some way for even the busiest parents among us to fit prayer into our day.

We are like the Apostles, who had the whole world waiting for the Good News Jesus sent them out to preach. Their days and nights were full, yet listen to what Jesus tells them:

The Apostles gathered together with Jesus and reported all they had done and taught. He said to them, "Come away by yourselves to a deserted place and rest a while." People were coming and going in great numbers, and they had no opportunity even to eat. So they went off in the boat by themselves to a deserted place. People saw them leaving and many came to know about it. They hastened there on foot from all the towns and arrived at the place before them.

When He disembarked and saw the vast crowd, His heart
was moved with pity for them, for they were like sheep without a shepherd; and He began to teach them many things.
(Mk 6:30-34)

Many spiritual writers, St. Ignatius chief among them,
recommend that we place ourselves in the Gospel scene as we
meditate upon it. We might first imagine ourselves as part of the
vast crowd taught by Jesus, but I think there is a greater similarity
between ourselves and the Apostles.

When we go to Jesus to tell Him all we have done and taught
in our homeschooling day, He does respond, "Come away by yourself . . . and rest awhile." It is all too often the case that the children of large Catholic families have been coming and going in great
numbers, and the mothers have no opportunity even to eat! But
while we need to eat and rest and occasionally take a shower, we
cannot live by bread alone, and we need also to nourish ourselves
with Heavenly food.

Jesus invites us to come away and rest with Him. Yes, the
children will often see us leaving, and hasten ahead of us to our
quiet place! But hopefully our spouses can help us to find this
necessary time of solitude, and at the very least we can—like the
Apostles—enjoy Our Lord's presence on the way. When the vast
crowd of our children or our obligations presses in upon us, we can
then be a little refreshed and ready again to work with Jesus.

We can make it our first priority to spend at least a few minutes with Him each day in quiet, letting Him show us who He is,
and who we are. A good beginning is to ask God for the grace to
want to spend time with Him. In the Sermon on the Mount, Jesus
assures us He will then take care of everything. He says, "Seek first
the kingdom, and all the rest will follow" (Luke 12:31). We also
read an affirmation of this truth in the Old Testament, "Delight
yourself in the Lord, and He will give you the desires of your heart"
(Psalm 37:4). Yet in our quest to know God as He truly is, we may
not know just where to begin.

Getting to Know God

The Heavenly Father shows us the Way. He has told us, "This is my Beloved Son; listen to Him" (Lk 9:35). As St. John of the Cross put it, "The Father spoke one Word, which was His Son. This Word He always speaks in eternal silence, and in silence must it be heard by the soul" (*Sayings of Light and Love*, §100). If we want to get to know God, and find our peace in Him, we must get to know His Son, His Word. Jesus Himself told us at the Last Supper, "I am the way, the truth, and the life. No one comes to the Father but through Me . . . . He who sees Me, sees also the Father" (John 14:6, 9).

We need to get to know Jesus in order to calm our souls, but there is another important reason for us, as Catholic parents, to increase our intimacy with Him. Our primary duty in our children's education is to pass on to them the Catholic faith, but passing on the Faith essentially amounts to sharing with them the knowledge and love of Jesus, our Savior. There is no replacement for our role as our children's first catechists. In *Catechesi Tradendae*, Pope John Paul II explained what this requires from us; namely, our own living knowledge of Jesus. He wrote:

> We must therefore say that in catechesis it is Christ, the Incarnate Word and Son of God, who is taught—everything else is taught with reference to Him—and it is Christ alone who teaches—anyone else teaches to the extent that he is Christ's spokesman, enabling Christ to teach with his lips. Whatever be the level of his responsibility in the Church, every catechist must constantly endeavor to transmit by his teaching and behavior the teaching and life of Jesus. He will not seek to keep directed towards himself and his personal opinions and attitudes the attention and the consent of the mind and heart of the person he is catechizing. Above all, he will not try to inculcate his personal opinions and options as if they expressed Christ's teaching and the lessons of His life. Every catechist should be able to apply to himself the mysterious words of Jesus: "My teaching is not mine, but His who sent Me." Saint Paul did this when he was dealing with a question of prime impor-

tance: "I received from the Lord what I also delivered to you."
What assiduous study of the word of God transmitted by the
Church's Magisterium, what profound familiarity with Christ
and with the Father, what a spirit of prayer, what detachment
from self must a catechist have in order that he can say: "My
teaching is not mine!" (§6)

There is a passage in the Church's morning prayer which always makes me think of this responsibility to know Jesus in order
to share Him with my children. In Psalm 48 we read:

Walk through Zion, walk all round it;
Count the number of its towers.
Review all its ramparts,
Examine its castles,
That you may tell the next generation
That such is our God,
Our God for ever and always.
It is He who leads us.

The Church explains in the psalm-prayer following Psalm 48:
"Father, the body of Your risen Son is the temple not made by
human hands and the defending wall of the new Jerusalem" (Thursday, Morning Prayer, Week I of the Divine Office). How privi-
leged we are to get to know Jesus, the Alpha and the Omega, the
beginning and end of all creation! What a joy to then introduce
our children to Him, the great Lover of their souls.

When we go to the Gospels to meet Jesus, and when we receive Him as our Divine Guest in Holy Communion, we find Him
ready to teach us exactly what we need to know. We cannot go
wrong, and we will begin to really know Him, when we take as our
starting point these words of His: "Learn from Me, for I am gentle
and humble of heart." How often do we misunderstand Jesus, because we forget to read the Gospels in the light of His gentleness?
If it seems simplistic to base our whole familiarity with Jesus on this
one verse, let us reflect on the entire discourse with which Jesus
introduces it. We read in the eleventh chapter of St. Matthew's
Gospel:

> At that time Jesus said in reply, "I give praise to You, Father, Lord of heaven and earth, for although You have hidden these things from the wise and the learned You have revealed them to the childlike. Yes, Father, such has been your gracious will. All things have been handed over to Me by my Father. No one knows the Son except the Father, and no one knows the Father except the Son and anyone to whom the Son wishes to reveal Him.
>
> "Come to Me, all you who labor and are burdened, and I will give you rest. Take my yoke upon you and learn from Me, for I am gentle and humble of heart; and you will find rest for your souls. For my yoke is easy, and my burden light." (Mt 11: 25-30; Luke adds that Jesus, as He said this, "rejoiced in the Holy Spirit." Cf. Lk 10: 21-22)

In our homeschooling, as in so many aspects of our life, we frequently burden ourselves with high expectations. We take on a yoke of our own making, and stumble under its weight. But Jesus wants us to take on His yoke, which He promises will be light. St. Thérèse of Lisieux, the Little Flower, said, "The Gospels are enough. I listen with delight to these words of Jesus which tell me what I must do: 'Learn of Me, for I am gentle and humble of heart;' then I am at peace, according to His sweet promise: 'And you will find rest for your little souls.'"

Taking St. Thérèse as our Guide

If we are looking for a sure guide to the knowledge of Jesus in His gentleness, we can do no better than to follow St. Thérèse. St. Thérèse of the Child Jesus and the Holy Face lived to be only twenty-four, dying in the Carmelite convent of Lisieux, France in 1897. Jesus has answered her prayers by letting her spend her heaven doing good on earth, and she specializes in helping us to learn about the merciful love of God. In October of 1997, on World Mission Sunday, Pope John Paul II declared her a Doctor of the Church. We cannot go astray by following her lead; the Church has assured us she is a safe guide in spiritual paths, and a trustworthy master in the science of love.

In the twenty years since St. Thérèse befriended me, I have discovered that relatively few authors are able to capture her spirit. I have read many books about her, and have often come away from them disappointed. There is one book, however, which never fails to awaken in me the confidence and love that are the hallmarks of St. Thérèse. This book is *I Believe in Love*, currently published by Sophia Institute Press. Written by Père Jean du Coeur de Jésus D'Elbée, a priest who remains otherwise unknown to us, *I Believe in Love* is a series of retreat conferences based on the teaching of St. Thérèse. My husband and I foist this book on almost everyone we meet, because it so effectively inspires knowledge and love of Jesus in all His gentleness.

Here is one of my favorite passages from *I Believe in Love*. I include it here as an introduction to the gentleness and love of Jesus. In our efforts to raise our children to be saints (which is the true goal of Catholic unschooling and all authentic Catholic education), let us learn to trust Jesus.

> I assure you, we are bathed in love and mercy. We each have a Father, a Brother, a Friend, a Spouse of our soul, Center and King of our hearts, Redeemer and Savior, bent down over us, over our weakness and our impotence, like that of little children, with an inexpressible gentleness, watching over us like the apple of His eye, who said, "I will have mercy and not sacrifice, for I have not come to call the just, but sinners" (Mt 9:13), a Jesus haunted by the desire to save us by all means, who has opened heaven under our feet. And we live, too often, like orphans, like abandoned children, as if it were hell which had opened under our feet. We are men of little faith! (p. 13)

Isn't it true that as Catholic homeschooling parents we can make the mistake of thinking that it is our job to save our children from hell, and give them the tools to "earn" heaven? We accidentally fall into Jansenist and Pelagian tendencies, forgetting that Jesus delights to save us, and He has earned Heaven for us. I find that

my problem in learning to trust centers on two erroneous assump-
tions; as soon as I reason away the first, the second rises up, and
then when the second is momentarily squashed, the first returns.
My two false principles are:

1. I think it all (my son's education, happiness, salvation . . .) depends on me.

2. I think I have to (and my son has to) achieve great things
   to please the world and, more importantly, to please God.

In the foregoing pages, we have provided the solution to my
quandary, for we have shown both these principles to be false. We
have seen that our children are natural learners and can be effective primary agents in their educations. As for their happiness and
salvation, we can provide them with the sacraments and prayer,
which are God's means to these ends. But what about achieving
great things? As I mentioned above, the world will be impressed
with the actual results of our children's learning. However, even if
they are not impressed, let's recall Mother Teresa's words: "We are
not called to be successful, but only to be faithful." Or, as a wise
friend used to tell me, "Success is not where it's at."

This leads us to ask the more important question; namely,
does God require us to achieve great things to please Him? Is it
part of being faithful to excel at what we do and how we do it? St.
Thérèse tells us very directly in her autobiography: "Jesus does not
demand great actions from us, but simply surrender and gratitude."
And again, "He has no need of our works, but only of our love"
(*Story of a Soul*, Chapter 9). I have discovered with her that God
does not ask all of us to be great. Psalm 131 puts these words on
our lips, which are recited as part of the Divine Office:

> O Lord, my heart is not proud
> Nor haughty my eyes.
> I have not gone after things too great
> Nor marvels beyond me.
> Truly I have set my soul

In silence and peace.
As a child has rest in its mother's arms,
Even so my soul.
O Israel, hope in the Lord
Both now and for ever.

Even when we have accepted that success is not our goal, we may have trouble setting our souls in silence and peace. Often we do not find consolation in Mother Teresa's words above, because we worry that we are not only not successful, but also not faithful. Then, with St. Thérèse, we must go a step further along the path of confidence in Jesus. She says, " I am not always faithful, but I never get discouraged. I abandon myself into the arms of Jesus and there I find again all that I have lost and much more besides" (Letter of July 18, 1893). What if, unlike Thérèse, we do get discouraged? Ah, our Saint always has the right words to reassure us. Here is one of my favorite of her sayings, in which she manages finally to undercut our persistent anxiety. She tells us: "Do not fear. The poorer you are, the more Jesus will love you. He will go far, very far in search of you, if at times you wander a little."

The more we get to know St. Thérèse, the more we see that she embraced the spirit of littleness in all things. We read in her *Last Conversations* that one day when she was standing in front of the convent library, she said to her sister Celine, "Oh! I would have been sorry to have read all those books!" Celine asked why, commenting, "This would have been quite an acquisition. I would understand your regretting to read them, but not to have already read them." Thérèse replied, "If I had read them, I would have broken my head, and I would have wasted precious time that I could have employed very simply in loving God" (p. 261).

As I have admitted already, I am a great lover of books and reading. I am hoping that Thérèse's remarks to Celine do not imply that these are always a waste of time! I think the important point is rather that St. Thérèse knew that God doesn't need our brilliance, our accomplishments, our excellence . . . . He desires only our love.

On another occasion, as Fr. Jamart relates in his book on Thérèse:

> One of her companions complained because she was not able to direct her will often to God. Thérèse reassured her: "That 'direction' is not necessary for those who are entirely dedicated to our Lord. No doubt, it is a good thing to recollect our mind, but we should do that gently, for constraint does not glorify the good Lord. He is well acquainted with the nice thoughts and the elegant expressions of love which we would like to address to Him, but He is satisfied with our desires. Is He not our Father and are we not His little children?" (*Complete Spiritual Doctrine of St. Thérèse of Lisieux*, p. 120)

I apply this passage to our parenting and homeschooling in the following manner. We can say that in these realms too we must proceed gently, that is with gentleness toward ourselves and our children. Moreover, it is equally true that constraint in these areas does not glorify the good Lord. Let us strive to realize that He is well acquainted with the good things we want to provide for our children, and that He is satisfied with our desires and our poor efforts. Is He not our Father and are we not His little children? We can stop pressuring ourselves to achieve success in our homeschooling, and apply ourselves instead to becoming "entirely dedicated to our Lord." Listen to what Thérèse wrote to her sister Leonie: "I assure you that God is even kinder than you think. He is satisfied with a look, a sigh of love." She would also have us remember that "He is all love, all tenderness."

It may take a lifetime to learn these lessons. Unfortunately we are not used to the gentleness of Jesus. As Father D'Elbée explains in *I Believe in Love*:

> Do you know what misleads us? The fact that the best men are often so hard. They grow tired of pardoning. They do not forget the wounds they may have received. The world is pitiless in its judgments . . . . We apply to the Heart of Jesus the measure of our own miserable little hearts, so mean, so nar-

row, so hard, and we do not succeed in comprehending how good, how indulgent, how compassionate, how gentle, how patient is Jesus himself. (p. 43)

For the children's sake, as well as our own, let us learn to know Jesus as He really is in Himself: indulgent, compassionate, gentle and patient. As we spend time with Him, He will help us to become like Him. We can repeat with Thérèse and her sister Leonie one of their favorite prayers, "Jesus, gentle and humble of heart, make my heart like unto thine."

Certainly we will again be attacked by scruples about our parenting and homeschooling efforts. But we must recognize such scruples as temptations, and seek to overcome them with patience and gentleness toward ourselves. The Church promises in the words of the Divine Office: "The gentle will inherit the earth. They will have peace to their hearts' content."

In the previous chapter we reviewed many of the reasons to trust nature, and these are important sources of support for unschoolers. Finally, though, the Catholic unschooler will gain confidence and peace by coming to know Jesus in all His gentleness. If we have much to look forward to in learning about creation, how much more do we have to look forward to in learning about Jesus, "in whom are hidden all the treasures of wisdom and knowledge" (Col 2:3)?

St. Paul writes in the letter to the Galatians: "For freedom Christ has set us free. Stand firm, then, and do not submit again to the yoke of slavery" (Gal 5:1). Catholic unschooling has allowed the freedom and joy of Christ to flourish in our home. I hope that some other families, too, will find in this approach the peace that Christ promises. As we have seen, unschooling requires that we learn to trust God, and learn to trust our children. We may think that we can never overcome our fears, and live with confidence, but we must remember, "With God, all things are possible" (Mt 19:26).

CHAPTER NINE:
BOOKS AS FRIENDS

> The familiar faces of my books welcomed me. I
> threw myself into my reading chair and gazed
> around me with pleasure. All my old friends
> present – there in spirit, ready to talk with me
> any moment when I was in the mood, making
> no claim upon my attention when I was not.
>
> -George MacDonald

Just as we need to learn to trust nature and learn to trust God, we need to surround ourselves with good friends in order to homeschool with peace. God has created us as social animals, and we cannot thrive without the support of some sort of community. When we choose a counter-cultural way of life like homeschooling, we may find ourselves alienated from extended family and friends, at least until they convince themselves that we haven't gone totally off the deep end! Although homeschooling is much more socially accept-able than it was twenty years ago, it can still be a lonely road to travel. The homeschooling mother thus needs to draw on as many sources of friendly support as she can.

Personality and temperament will play a role in what kind of support is most supportive for any particular mom. For some moth-ers, the best source of encouragement may be a local homeschooling support group and the friendships it nourishes. I know women who enjoy a monthly night out with girlfriends; others get together for an evening book group once a month. Another friend of mine prefers a Saturday "retreat" spent off on her own shopping, and going to a Vigil Mass while her husband watches the kids. There are even many vibrant communties of homeschooling mothers who find like-minded friends on the internet, getting the support they need without leaving their homes.

In my own homeschooling life, I cherish above all the irreplaceable support my husband offers, and our older son Joseph is a valued companion. Baby Dominic provides the spontaneous affection and joy which brightens my days at unexpected moments. I also thank God for the many supportive relatives and friends with which He has blessed me, and the community of Catholic homeschoolers into which He has placed me.

I must admit, however, that my support system would be incomplete without the friendship that I have found in books. Lacordaire, the great French Dominican preacher, is reputed to have said, "Only three things are necessary to make life happy: the blessing of God, books, and a friend." I would add that in a pinch, when the friend is not available, the blessing of God and books might just be enough for earthly happiness! What I really want to explain is that like many book-lovers before me, I have discovered that the books themselves become cherished friends.

In this chapter, then, I conclude my reflections on Catholic unschooling with a paean in praise of books. You may already count books as some of your closest friends, and then you can sing along with me. If, though, you haven't yet considered books as friends, I urge you to begin looking to them for solace and camaraderie on your homeschooling journey. Once you make the acquaintance of a few good books, it will be the most natural thing in the world to introduce them to your children. And then you will find that these new friends are faithful and true, for they will bring comfort and pleasure to you and your children for many years to come.

Books as Treasures

As I have mentioned already in these pages, we are a family of book lovers. To be more precise, we are a family of readers, and my love of books has provided us with a constant supply of things to read. Since our small family size has allowed me the leisure to browse all new and used bookstores within my reach for the last fifteen years, we have built up quite a library. More importantly, my book hunting has unearthed many treasures that have enriched our lives.

Books are nearly inexhaustible sources of information, knowledge, and even wisdom. As such they play a large role in our unschooling, and have been a wonderful instrument in Joseph's education thus far. From encyclopedias to comic books to novels, a great variety of literature has passed through our home, and his hands. We have definitely been selective, choosing for our family only what we consider noble, good, or just clean fun, and rejecting the base, vulgar, or otherwise unworthy material that we've come across.

While books have been useful for learning things, they have been so much more to us than tools. They have allowed us to laugh together, to think through dilemmas, to explore faraway places, to meet heroes of the past. When Joseph was four, and we drove for hours on a summer trip, I read the Narnia Chronicles to him. (I don't think he understood very much, but I really loved reading the whole series for the first time). When at age nine he was sick with the chicken pox, I distracted him with Hilda Van Stockum's Bantry Bay trilogy. And over the years when we visited Grandma and Grandpa, he raided Grandpa's store of Pogo comics. In each of these situations, and so many more, books have been for us sources of comfort and friendship, the truest kind of treasure.

In the following passage, Elizabeth Goudge, who has become one of my favorite authors, explains why books can be so dear:

> The sources of our comfort are legion, and cannot be counted, but if we attempted the impossible and tried to make a list most of us would place books very high indeed, perhaps second only to faith, for reading is not only a pleasure in itself, with its concomitants of stillness, quietness and forgetfulness of self, but in what we read many of our other comforts are present with us like reflections seen in a mirror. If the light of our faith flickers we can make it steady again by reading of the faith of the saints, and hearing poetry sing to us the songs of

the lovers of God. In the absence of children we can read
about them, and in the cold and darkness of mid-winter look
in the mirror of our book and see flowers and butterflies, and
spring passing into the glow and warmth of summer. (From
the Preface to A *Book of Comfort*)

Books as Friends

While I think of books as treasures, I consider them also, along
with their authors and even their characters, as friends. Perhaps it
is not surprising that we should feel friendship for certain authors.
After all, they are trying to communicate to us through their writing. When we discover in books various thoughts, opinions, and
sentiments that agree with our own, we claim their authors as soul-
mates. The barriers of time and place are overcome, and our loneliness is lightened. This may seem most obvious when we read
non-fiction, but let's not forget the countless readers who have felt
a close kinship with Jane Austen, for example, when they have
discovered her six novels.

One of the most amusing and wonderful tricks of an author is
to put this kind of friendship for another author into a novel. The
first time Joseph and I ran across this together was in the books of
Edward Eager. He was a great admirer of E. Nesbit, and led us to
discover her too. In Eager's *Half Magic*, the children "had found
some books by a writer named E. Nesbit, surely the most wonderful books in the world. They read every one that the library had,
right away, except a book called *The Enchanted Castle*, which had
been out." You can bet that Joseph and I went back to the library
(where we had checked out *Half Magic*) to find *The Enchanted
Castle* ourselves, and luckily for us it was on the shelf!

Elizabeth Goudge also likes to give her characters good taste
in literature. In *The Scent of Water*, Elizabeth Goudge has the main
character, Mary, keep a volume of Jane Austen by her bed. "She
liked Jane. She liked her cheerful sanity. She [Jane] had expected

no very great things of human nature, yet she had loved it, and in
Mr. Knightley and Jane Bennett she had portrayed a quiet steady
goodness that had been as lasting in literature as it would have
been in life."

What could Joseph and I feel toward the children in *Half
Magic*, except profound gratitude for introducing us to E. Nesbit?
And how could I help but feel friendly toward Mary when I discovered that we both love Jane Austen? We are open hearted people,
and in welcoming books into our homes, we have forged friendships with the authors and their characters. After a while, since
we love to re-read our old favorites, the books themselves become
our friends. As Hugh Walpole tells us in *Reading, An Essay*:

> There is a kind of luxury of laziness in Reading which is per-
> haps the best thing in all the world; it is to be captured only, I
> think, through the old books, books that you know so well
> that they step out and meet you, take you by the arm and
> whisper in your ear: 'Now lie back and talk to us, and then we
> will in our turn tell you a thing or two. There's no need to be
> clever this evening, we don't want you to shine, we'll have an
> hour or two together so pleasant that you'll scarcely know we're
> here.'
> As now in retrospect I look back I can find so many books
> that have in this way been my friends that their number is past
> all counting.

The Booklists: A Matter of Taste

This passage leads perfectly to what I now need to explain. Books
have been such a central feature of our Catholic unschooling, and
have been such a help to us along our way thus far, that this book
would not be complete without the booklists you will find in the
appendices. In presenting you with these lists, I am actually introducing you to some of my best friends, and I am a little nervous
about how you will all get along. To put this another way, reverting
back to the idea of books as treasures, I agree with Elizabeth Goudge

that "the sharing can cause trepidation as well as pleasure for what is treasure for oneself is not always treasure for other people. Their hoard would have been very different and they will think yours an odd mixture" (from the Preface to *A Book of Comfort*).

I am reminded of the night that I met with a group of ladies to discuss a novel they had read on my recommendation. I was initially distressed that none of them liked the book, but my dismay soon turned to amusement. Everyone had a different reason for hating the book, and in the end my poor author was found guilty on every possible count! Since I considered this one of the best books I'd ever read, and the ladies were good friends, I decided to fall back on the adage, "There is no accounting for taste." (No, I will not name the author and his book, for fear that I would prejudice you against them!)

I will excuse my lists by saying with Hugh Walpole, "As this . . . is to be concerned, I believe, with the pleasures of Reading it can be nothing if it is not autobiographical, for the only certain thing about Reading is that it is personal first, personal second, and personal all the time, and Milton's *Paradise Lost* and Dante's *Divina Comedia* may be the twin dominating peaks of a glorious range, but they are nothing to you whatever if you happen to be looking the other way."

I am not saying that there are no true standards for good literature. But my standards in the pages which follow have been more according to good morals and what I consider good taste— namely my own! I am fairly confident that you will find friends here: some old friends to be met with again and introduced to your children, others that you may meet now for the first time, but soon will come to know and love.

Principles of Selection

We are a family of sensitive plants. Consequently my list for parents contains "Novels I can read." There are lots of great novels which I have read and enjoyed once upon a time, but I find that as I get older I appreciate only the gentle touch. The novels listed here have passed my test of no harshness and no edginess. Our recommended children's books are also free of the sarcastic modern tone, and as much as possible free of any other "bad stuff" too.

Our discussions with Joseph about what is worth reading, as well as his steady diet of wholesome pleasant books, have helped him to develop his own sensitivity to good literature, and his personal desire to avoid anything bad. His ability to discern has served us well, because there came a time years ago when my reading couldn't keep pace with his; I needed to trust him to tell me if a book I provided for him turned out to be objectionable. I could no longer pre-read all that I gave him, and fortunately I didn't need to by that time. In other words, I have become dependent upon his good judgment to help me select our books.

Joseph and I have worked together to pare down our lists. I have had trouble using other people's booklists in the past, because they were too long for me and I didn't know where to begin. Apparently, this has been a problem throughout human history, since we read in the Old Testament: "Of making books there is no end, and much study is a weariness of the flesh" (Eccles 12:12). We realized that if we were to include on our list every interesting author in alphabetical order, you might never meet "Van Stockum, Hilda," and that would be a shame. Thus we've tried to limit ourselves to our best friends among the books. Wonderful authors and books have been left off our list, because they didn't rank among those that most captured our fancy.

Following the booklists I have provided a list of book suppliers, along with their website addresses and phone numbers. We want to make it as easy as possible for you to find our friends, the books.

The Problem of Age-Levels

It is hard to give age levels for books. Recently I came across an essay by Chesterton in which he argued that there is no proper category of "children's books." He thought that books which genuinely appeal to children should appeal to adults too, and I must say that this has been my experience. As I write, Joseph is reminding me that Tolkien says fairy tales aren't just for kids. If we look at it from the other direction, however, there are good books which I have saved for Joseph to enjoy at a later date; not every good book needs to be read now. Some children will be ready for some books earlier or later than other children are.

A further complication in assigning age levels is the distinction between books which are read aloud to a child, and books the child reads on his own. Usually those read aloud to the child can be much more complex in style and content than those he can read by himself. Later, the child will likely revisit on his own the books that were favorite read alouds in his younger days. Most of the books on our read aloud list Joseph later read to himself. Don't be afraid to experiment with read alouds; your children will let you know if the books you choose aren't the right ones! Or perhaps you will notice that it seems like hard work for all of you to follow along, in which case you can switch to lighter fare.

I encourage you to continue to read aloud as a family long after your children are all independent readers. Jim Trelease has written a whole book on the benefits of reading aloud called *The Read Aloud Handbook*. You will form close bonds with your children by entering the world of books together over the years. As Joseph says, "Any really good book would be great to read aloud. *The Lord of the Rings* doesn't seem like a book to read aloud, does it? And it was great reading aloud."

In our lists, I have attempted to solve the problem of age levels by dividing the children's books into the broad categories of those for "little ones," "young readers," and "older children." These are meant to correspond roughly to pre-readers/beginning readers, younger readers, and older readers. The break between these last two may be around eleven to thirteen years old, but again I hesitate to set down exact ages. In this last year, at age twelve to thirteen, Joseph has been reading P. G. Wodehouse and G. K. Chesterton novels for the first time, but yesterday I caught him with some old Mickey Mouse comic books, and today he is immersed in the continuing adventures of *The Happy Hollisters*. There are no hard and fast rules for reading enjoyment!

A FINAL WORD

In this book I have argued that Catholic unschooling makes sense, in terms of both nature and grace. By thinking through and articulating the homeschooling style that works for us, I have tried to assuage fears and instill trust: for myself, and for any interested readers as well.

I have it on good authority (namely, from everyone whose children are grown) that these years with our children will go so quickly. Before we know it, our homeschooling years will be behind us, and our children will be well on their way to raising children of their own. Let's enjoy the precious time we have as homeschooling parents, and learn to relax with our kids. Along with a glass of wine, or a cozy mug of hot chocolate, curl up with one of the good books we recommend. Draw your children close, and thank God for His kindness. Heed Jesus' gentle admonition, and do not be afraid, for truly, your Father is pleased to give you the Kingdom.

APPENDIX A:
A BOOKLIST FOR PARENTS

For Refreshment
For Unschooling/Homeschooling
For Growth in Trust

FOR REFRESHMENT

Authors Whose Novels I Can Read

Alcott, Louisa May
Little Women
Eight Cousins
Rose in Bloom

Austen, Jane
Pride and Prejudice
Sense and Sensibility
Emma
Mansfield Park
Persuasion
Northanger Abbey

Benson, E. F.
Queen Lucia (series)

Cather, Willa
Shadows on the Rock
Death Comes for the Archbishop

Goudge, Elizabeth
The Scent of Water
The Dean's Watch
The Rosemary Tree
The Little White Horse
The Bird in the Tree
Pilgrim's Inn
The Heart of the Family

Jewett, Sarah Orne
The Country of the Pointed Firs

Karon, Jan
At Home in Mitford (series)

Montgomery, L. M.
Anne of Green Gables (series)

Morley, Christopher
Parnassus on Wheels
The Haunted Bookshop

Porter, Gene Stratton
Freckles
A Girl of the Limberlost
Laddie
The Song of the Cardinal
The Harvester

Stevenson, D. E.
Miss Buncle's Book
Miss Buncle Married

Tarkington, Booth
Penrod
Seventeen
Gentle Julia
The Flirt
Rumbin Galleries
Image of Josephine

Trollope, Anthony
The Warden
Barchester Towers

Wodehouse, P. G.
Any and all titles!
I really like *Something New*

Essays and Humor

Milne, A. A.
Not That it Matters
A Table Near the Band

Thurber, James
My Life and Hard Times
The Thurber Carnival

White, E. B.
Essays
The Elements of Style (with William Strunk)

My Favorite English Catholic Authors

Baring, Maurice
The Puppet Show of Memory
The Coat Without Seam

Belloc, Hilaire
A Path to Rome

Benson, Robert Hugh
The Friendship of Christ
Loneliness?

Chesterton, G. K.
What's Wrong with the World

Guinness, Sir Alec
Blessings in Disguise
My Name Escapes Me

Knox, Ronald
Pastoral and Occasional Sermons
Retreat for Lay People

Pearce, Joseph
Literary Converts

Waugh, Evelyn
Scoop
Brideshead Revisited

Poetry

Browning, Elizabeth Barrett

Frost, Robert

Hopkins, Gerard Manley

Patmore, Coventry
The Angel in the House

The Neumann Press Book of Verse

FOR UNSCHOOLING/HOMESCHOOLING

Books by John Holt
How Children Fail
How Children Learn
Learning All the Time
Teach Your Own (with Patrick Farenga)
Never Too Late
Growing Without Schooling: A Record of a Grassroots Movement
    (contains the first 12 issues of Holt's newsletter/magazine)

Friends and Followers of John Holt

Wallace, Nancy
Better Than School
Child's Work

McKee, Alison
Homeschooling Our Children, Unschooling Ourselves

In the Unschooling Mood

Colfax, David & Micki
Homeschooling for Excellence
Hard Times in Paradise

Gatto, John Taylor
Dumbing Us Down: The Invisible Curriculum of Compulsory Schooling
The Underground History of American Education

Hailey, Kendall
The Day I Became an Autodidact

More Helpful Homeschooling Books

Hood, Mary
(Christian/Relaxed Homeschooling)
The Relaxed Home School
The Joyful Home Schooler
Taking the Frustration out of Math (booklet)

Levison, Catherine
A Charlotte Mason Education

McCauley, Susan Schaeffer
(Christian/Charlotte Mason approach)
For the Children's Sake

Beechik, Ruth
(Christian/gentle guidelines for what to know when)
The 3 R's

Moore, Raymond & Dorothy
(Christian; among the earliest homeschool advocates)
Home Style Teaching; and others

Catholic Homeschooling Books

Clark, Mary Kay
Catholic Homeschooling

Berquist, Laura
Designing Your Own Classical Curriculum

Hahn, Kimberly & Hasson, Mary
Catholic Education: Homeward Bound

Mackson, Rachel & Wittmann, Maureen
A Catholic Homeschool Treasury

Foss, Elizabeth
Real Learning: Education in the Heart of the Home

Books on Books

Bennett, William Rose
The Reader's Encyclopedia

Hanff, Helene
84, Charing Cross Road

O'Brien, Michael D.
A Landscape with Dragons

Fagan, Theresa
A Mother's List of Books (booklet)

Trelease, Jim
The Read Aloud Handbook

FOR GROWTH IN TRUST

The Bible

As a learned priest once taught me, the Church reads the Bible as liturgy. To enter into the Church's liturgy, try using a Missal and the Divine Office. Even if you aren't able to make it to weekday Mass, you can read along with the Liturgy of the Word throughout the Liturgical Year at home, and/or join in the Liturgy of the Hours.

For a convenient and current Missal, you might like the monthly *Magnificat*. It costs about $40 for a one-year subscription. Their website is www.magnificat.net or call (800) 317-6689.

The Divine Office is available in a one-volume edition (without the complete Office of Readings) from Pauline Books and Media. They also sell a separate volume containing the complete Office of Readings.

Scripture Passages for Growth in Trust

Psalms:	19, 23, 27, 33, 34, 42, 45, 46, 48, 62, 63, 65, 81, 84, 92, 100, 103, 113, 116, 125, 127, 130, 131, 139, 146, 147
Song of Songs	
Isaiah	especially: 12; 30:15-26; 35; 40-46; 49-55; 58; 60-66
The Gospels	especially: John 14-17
Romans	8
1 Corinthians	1-2; 12-13
2 Corinthians	10; 12:1-10
Galatians	5
Ephesians	
Philippians	
Colossians	3
Hebrews	1; 4; 12; 13
1 Peter	
1 John	especially: 4

St. Thérèse Books

Books by her
Story of a Soul: The Autobiography of St. Thérèse of Lisieux
The Letters of St. Thérèse of Lisieux and Those Who Knew Her, General Correspondence: Volume II

Compilations
Thoughts of St. Thérèse (TAN)
The Little Way of St. Thérèse of Lisieux, ed. John Nelson

Books about her

D'Elbée, Fr. Jean du Couer de Jésus
I Believe in Love

Liagre, Père
A Retreat with St. Thérèse

Jamart, Francois
Complete Spiritual Doctrine of St. Thérèse of Lisieux

Books about Her Sisters, and Their Paths Down the Little Way

Piat, Stephane-Joseph
Celine

Baudouin-Croix
Leonie Martin: A Difficult Life

Descouvement, Pierre
Thérèse of Lisieux and Marie of the Trinity

FOR YOUNG FOLK

APPENDIX B:
A BOOKLIST FOR CHILDREN

Our Favorite Read Alouds
Books for Little Ones
Books for Young Readers
Books for Older Children

WHEN MOTHER READS ALOUD

When Mother reads aloud, the past
    Seems real as every day;
I hear the tramp of armies vast,
I see the spears and lances cast,
    I join the trilling fray;
Brave knights and ladies fair and proud
I meet when Mother reads aloud.

When Mother reads aloud, far lands
    Seem very near and true;
I cross the desert's gleaming sands,
Or hunt the jungle's prowling bands,
    Or sail the ocean blue.
Far heights, whose peaks the cold mists shroud,
I scale, when Mother reads aloud.

When Mother reads aloud, I long,
    For noble deeds to do—
To help the right, redress the wrong;
It seems so easy to be strong,
    So simple to be true.
Oh, thick and fast the visions crowd
My eyes, when Mother reads aloud.

                                    -Unknown

OUR FAVORITE READ ALOUDS
(IN ORDER OF APPEARANCE)

Milne, A. A.
Winnie the Pooh

Atwater, Richard & Florence
Mr. Popper's Penguins

Barrie, J. M.
Peter Pan

Bond, Michael
A Bear Called Paddington

Kastner, Erich
Emil and the Detectives

Dahl, Roald
Charlie and the Chocolate Factory

Lewis, C. S.
The Narnia Chronicles (series)

Baum, L. Frank
The Wonderful Wizard of Oz

Sidney, Margaret
The Five Little Peppers and How They Grew

Tolkien, J. R. R.
The Hobbit

White, E. B.
Charlotte's Web

Haywood, Carolyn
Little Eddie
Eddie and His Big Deals

Cleary, Beverly
Ramona the Pest
Henry Huggins
Ribsy

MacDonald, Betty
Mrs. Piggle Wiggle (series)

Brink, Carol Ryrie
The Pink Motel
Caddie Woodlawn

Hale, Lucretia P.
The Peterkin Papers

Thurber, James
The Thirteen Clocks

Eager, Edward
Half Magic

Nesbit, E.
The Enchanted Castle
The Story of the Treasure Seekers
The Wouldbegoods

Winthrop, Elizabeth
The Castle in the Attic

Enright, Elizabeth
The Saturdays

Estes, Eleanor
Ginger Pye

Tolkien, J. R. R.
The Lord of the Rings (trilogy)

Wyss, Johannes
Swiss Family Robinson

Tarkington, Booth
Penrod: His Complete Story
Gentle Julia

Verne, Jules
Around the World in Eighty Days

MacDonald, George
The Princess and the Goblin
The Princess and Curdie

Wodehouse, P. G.
Leave it to Psmith

THE LAND OF STORY BOOKS

At evening when the lamp is lit,
Around the fire my parents sit;
They sit at home and talk and sing,
And do not play at anything.

Now, with my little gun, I crawl
All in the dark along the wall,
And follow round the forest track
Away behind the sofa back.

There, in the night, where none can spy,
All in my hunter's camp I lie,
And play at books that I have read
Till it is time to go to bed.

These are the hills, these are the woods,
These are my starry solitudes;
And there the river by whose brink
The roaring lions come to drink.

I see the others far away
As if in firelit camp they lay,
And I, like to an Indian scout,
Around their party prowled about.

So, when my nurse comes in for me,
Home I return across the sea,
And go to bed with backward looks
At my dear Land of Story Books.
                    -Robert Louis Stevenson

BOOKS FOR LITTLE ONES

Arnold, Mary
The Fussy Angel

Bemelmans, Ludwig
Madeline (series)

Benson, Robert Hugh
An Alphabet of Saints

Berenstain, Stan & Jan:
The Berenstain Bears (series)

Berger, Barbara
The Donkey's Dream

Bond, Michael
A Bear Called Paddington (series)
The Tales of Olga da Polga (series)

Burgess, Thornton
The Adventures of . . . Reddy Fox
                      . . . Poor Mrs. Quack
                      . . . etc. (series)
Mother West Wind Stories

De Brunhoff, Jean
Babar (series)

DePaola, Tomie
The Art Lesson

Eastman, P. D.
Are You My Mother?

Hodges, Margaret
Saint George and the Dragon
The Kitchen Knight

Hoff, Syd
Danny and the Dinosaur

McCloskey, Robert
Blueberries for Sal
Make Way for Ducklings

Milne, A. A.
Winnie the Pooh
The House at Pooh Corner
When We Were Very Young
Now We Are Six

Minarik, Else Holmelund
Little Bear (series)

Parrish, Peggy
Amelia Bedelia (series)

Peterson, John
The Littles (series)

Potter, Beatrix
The Tale of Peter Rabbit (series)

Rey, H. A.
Curious George (series)

Scarry, Richard
Cars and Trucks and Things that Go
Busy, Busy World

Seuss, Dr.
Hop on Pop
Fox in Socks
I am not Going to Get Up Today

Stevenson, Robert Louis
A Child's Garden of Verses

Taylor, Mark
Henry the Explorer

Titus, Eve
Anatole (series)

Van Stockum, Hilda
The Angel's Alphabet

Zion, Gene
Harry the Dirty Dog (series)

BOOKS FOR YOUNG READERS (Ages 7-12)

History (Secular Biography)

Joseph has enjoyed the **Landmark series** history books. These were popular hardcover children's books on individual historical figures and episodes, published in the 1950's. They can be found in used book stores in original hardcover; they are also being reprinted in paperback. Some of Joseph's favorites are:

Adams, Samuel Hopkins
The Pony Express

Blassingame, Wyatt
The French Foreign Legion

Kuhn, Ferdinand
The Story of the Secret Service

Reeder, Colonel Red
The West Point Story

Reynolds, Quentin
The F. B. I.

Religious Biography (Saints)

We have enjoyed the **Vision series** published by Ignatius Press, and the **Mary Fabyan Windeatt series** published by TAN. Although they are now out of print, Joseph especially liked the Daughters of St. Paul's **Encounter Books**. Some favorites are:

Gardiner, Harold C.
Edmund Campion: Hero of God's Underground

Daughters of St. Paul
Ahead of the Crowd: The Story of Dominic Savio

Daughters of St. Paul
God's Secret Agent: The Life of Michael Augustine Pro, S.J.

General Non-fiction

Bendick, Jeanne
Archimedes and the Door of Science
Galen and the Gateway to Medicine

Land of our Lady history series
Founders of Freedom (Vol. I)
Bearers of Freedom (Vol. II)

Nevins, Fr. Albert J.
Our American Catholic Heritage

Peet, Bill
An Autobiography

Schick, I. T. (ed.)
Battledress, The Uniforms of the World's Great Armies

Wiker, Benjamin D.
The Mystery of the Periodic Table

Fiction for Young Readers

Alcott, Louisa May
Little Women
Little Men
Jack and Jill

Appleton, Victor
Tom Swift (series)

Atwater, Richard & Florence
Mr. Popper's Penguins

Arthur, Robert
The Three Investigators (series)

Banks, Lynne Reid
I, Houdini
The Indian in the Cupboard

Barrie, J. M.
Peter Pan

Baum, L. Frank
The Wonderful Wizard of Oz (series)

Bianco, Margery
Forward, Commandos!

Bishop, Claire H.
Twenty and Ten

Blyton, Enid
The Magic, Faraway Tree
The Folk of the Faraway Tree
Famous Five series: *Five on a Treasure Island*, etc.
Secret Seven series

Bond, Michael
A Bear Called Paddington (series)
Olga da Polga (series)

Brill, Ethel C.
Madeline Takes Command

Brink, Carol Ryrie
The Pink Motel
Caddie Woodlawn
Baby Island

Brinley, Bertrand R.
The Mad Scientists' Club
The New Adventures of the Mad Scientists' Club

Brooks, Walter R.
Freddy the Detective (series)

Burnford, Sheila
The Incredible Journey

Butterworth, Oliver
The Enormous Egg
The Trouble with Jenny's Ear
The Narrow Passage

Cameron, Eleanor
The Wonderful Flight to the Mushroom Planet (series)

Carroll, Lewis
Alice in Wonderland and Through the Looking Glass

Cleary, Beverly
Ramona the Pest (series; but we skipped *Ramona and her Father*, and
Ramona and her Mother)
The Mouse and the Motorcycle (series)
Otis Spofford
Ellen Tibbets
Henry Huggins (series)

Corbett, Scott
The Lemonade Trick

Dahl, Roald
(some of his are very odd; we love these three)
Charlie and the Chocolate Factory
Charlie and the Great Glass Elevator
James and the Giant Peach

Daly, Maureen
The Small War of Sergeant Donkey

Defoe, Daniel
Robinson Crusoe

DeJong, Meindert
The Wheel on the School
The House of Sixty Fathers

du Bois, William Pène:
The Twenty-One Balloons
Giant
The Three Policemen

Dixon, Frank W.
The Hardy Boys series (we skipped *The Witchmaster's Key* and edited
Mystery of the Aztec Warrior)

Eager, Edward
Knight's Castle
Magic or Not
The Time Garden

Enright, Elizabeth
The Saturdays (Melendy Family series)
Gone-Away Lake
Return to Gone-Away Lake

Erickson, John R.
Hank the Cowdog (series)

Estes, Eleanor
The Moffats (series)
Ginger Pye

Fisher, Dorothy Canfield
Understood Betsy

Fleming, Ian
Chitty-Chitty Bang Bang

French, Allen
The Red Keep
The Lost Baron
The Story of Rolf and the Viking Bow

Gannett, Ruth S.
My Father's Dragon (series)

Garfield, James B.
Follow My Leader

George, Jean
My Side of the Mountain

Godden, Rumer
The Kitchen Madonna

Hale, Lucretia P.
The Peterkin Papers

Haywood, Carolyn
Little Eddie (series)
B is for Betsy (series)

Hergé
Tintin (series; comic books)

Hicks, Clifford B.
Alvin Fernald, Superweasel (series)

Juster, Norton
The Phantom Tollbooth

Kastner, Erich
Emil and the Detectives
The Little Man

Kelly, Walt
Pogo (series; comic books)

Kendall, Carol
The Gammage Cup
The Whisper of Glocken

Kipling, Rudyard
The Jungle Books
Just So Stories

Konigsberg, E. L.
From the Mixed Up Files of Mrs. Basil E. Frankweiler

Lang, Andrew
The Chronicles of Pantouflia

Laurence, Margaret
Jason's Quest

Lawson, Robert
Rabbit Hill
The Tough Winter

Lewis, C. S.
The Lion, The Witch, and the Wardrobe
(The Narnia Chronicles series)

Lindgren, Astrid
Pippi Longstocking (series)
The Children of Noisy Village
Ronia, the Robber's Daughter

Lofting, Hugh
The Voyages of Dr. Dolittle (series)

MacDonald, Betty
Mrs. Piggle Wiggle (series)

MacDonald, George
The Princess and the Goblin
The Princess and Curdie

MacGregor, Ellen
Miss Pickerell Goes to the Arctic (series)

Madigan, Leo
The Weka-Feather Cloak

McCloskey, Robert
Homer Price
Centerburg Tales

McSwigan, Marie
Snow Treasure

Merrill, Jean
The Pushcart War
The Toothpaste Millionaire

Montgomery, L. M.
Anne of Green Gables

Morey, Walt
Gentle Ben

Mowat, Farley
The Dog Who Wouldn't Be
Owls in the Family

Nesbit, E.
The Enchanted Castle
The Book of Dragons
The Story of the Treasure Seekers (series)
The Railway Children
Beautiful Stories from Shakespeare for Children

North, Sterling
Rascal

O'Brien, Robert C.
Mrs. Frisby and the Rats of N.I.M.H.

Pellowski, Anne
First Farm in the Valley: Anna's Story
(Polish American Girls series)

Porter, Eleanor H.
Pollyanna

Reilly, Robert
Red Hugh, Prince of Donegal

Robertson, Keith
Henry Reed, Inc. (series)

Selden, George
The Cricket in Times Square (series)

Seredy, Kate
The Good Master
The Singing Tree
The White Stag

Serraillier, Ian
Escape from Warsaw (original title: *The Silver Sword*)

Sharp, Margery
Miss Bianca (Rescuers series)

Sidney, Margaret
Five Little Peppers and How They Grew

Sobol, Donald J.
Encyclopedia Brown (series)
Secret Agents Four

Spyri, Johanna
Heidi

Styles, Showell
Midshipman Quinn Collection
The Flying Ensign

Sutcliffe, Rosemary
The Eagle of the Ninth
The Silver Branch
The Lantern Bearers
The Shining Company

Thurber, James
The Thirteen Clocks
The Wonderful O

Titus, Eve
Basil of Baker Street (series)

Tolkien, J. R. R.
The Hobbit
Farmer Giles of Ham

Van Stockum, Hilda
The Winged Watchman
The Mitchells: Five for Victory
Canadian Summer
Friendly Gables
The Cottage at Bantry Bay
Francie on the Run
Pegeen

Wallace, Sister Imelda
Outlaws of Ravenhurst

Warner, Gertrude Chandler
The Boxcar Children (series; but not those "created by" her)

West, Jerry
The Happy Hollisters (series)

White, E. B.
Charlotte's Web
(we didn't like the ending to *Stuart Little*)

White, T. H.
The Sword in the Stone
Mistress Masham's Repose

Winterfeld, Henry
Detectives in Togas
Mystery of the Roman Ransom

Winthrop, Elizabeth
The Castle in the Attic

Wyss, Johannes
Swiss Family Robinson

BOOKS FOR OLDER CHILDREN

This is a much shorter list, because we've only recently begun to explore this category with Joseph.

Fiction

Chesterton, G. K.
The Innocence of Father Brown (series)
Tales of the Long Bow
The Man Who Knew Too Much
The Paradoxes of Mr. Pond
Man Alive
The Ball and the Cross
Four Faultless Felons
The Club of Queer Trades
The Man Who Was Thursday
The Napoleon of Notting Hill
The Flying Inn

Doyle, Arthur Conan
Sherlock Holmes (series, except *The Sign of the Four*)

Guareschi, Giovanni
The Little World of Don Camillo (series)

Jacques, Brian
Redwall (series)

Tarkington, Booth
Penrod: His Complete Story

Thurber, James
My Life and Hard Times

Tolkien, J. R. R.
The Lord of the Rings
The Silmarillion

Trevor, Mariol
The Crystal Snowstorm
Following the Phoenix
Angel and Dragon
The Rose and Crown

Verne, Jules
20,000 Leagues Under the Sea

Wodehouse, P. G.
Psmith in the City
Psmith Journalist
Leave it to Psmith
The World of Mr. Mulliner

Zahn, Timothy
Star Wars novels (Laura Berquist enjoyed these too):
Heir to the Empire
Dark Force Rising
The Last Command
Specter of the Past
Vision of the Future

APPENDIX C:
BOOK SUPPLIERS

Where To Find Our Friends,
Once You Know Their Names

I have listed all books by author, with last name first, so that you will be prepared to locate these treasures. Here are the places I recommend you look when you are ready to find the books:

1. Your local public library, including all local branches and inter-library loan.
2. Your local bookstore, whether small or mega; both will special order if the books you want are not in stock, but are in print. Some provide search services if the book is out of print.
3. Websites; for out of print books try abe.com
4. Catalogues (printed and/or online) from publishers and homeschooling family businesses. My favorites are:

a. **Emmanuel Books,** with lots of Catholic resources, run by Lawrence and Paola Ciskanik. Find them at www.emmanuelbooks.com or call (800) 871-5598.

b. **Bethlehem Books** has wonderful children's books. They publish excellent historical fiction and captivating adventure stories, among other things. You can see their selection at **www.bethlehembooks.com** or call them at (800) 757-6831.

c. **FUN Books**, an unschooling catalogue with lots of good stuff, including books by John Holt and back issues of *Growing Without Schooling*. Their website is www.FUN-Books.com or request a print catalogue by calling (888) FUN-7020.

d. **Preserving Christian Publications**, specializing in out of print Catholic books. Their complete inventory can be seen at www.pcpbooks.com or call (866) 241-2762 for a print catalogue of their latest selections.

e. **Ignatius Press**, which carries Bethlehem Books for children, and has a terrific assortment of books for grown-ups too. They also carry Catholic art and videos. Check www.ignatius.com or call (800) 651-1531.

f. **TAN Books and Publishing, Inc.** reprints many great books; check their website at www.tanbooks.com or call them at: (800) 437-5876.

g. **The Institute of Carmelite Studies/ICS Publications** specializes in the writings of the Carmelite Saints; they give a 40% discount if you order five or more books at once; try www.icspublications.org or call them at (800) 832-8489.

h. **Pauline Books and Media**, run by the Daughters of St. Paul, has a website at www.pauline.org or call (800) 876-4463.

i. **Alba House**, run by the Fathers and Brothers of the Society of St. Paul, has a website at www.albahouse.org or call (800) 343-2522.

j. **Sophia Institute Press**, publisher of *I Believe in Love*, can be found at www.sophiainstitute.com or call (800) 888-9344.

k. **Dover** publishes tons of inexpensive classics for all ages and tastes; plus stationary, music scores, and more. Check their website at www.doverpublications.com for a complete list of books.

l. **The Neumann Press** reprints high quality Catholic books for children and adults. Their website can be found at www.neumannpress.com or call (800) 746-2521.

m. **The Elijah Company** carries books by relaxed homeschooler Mary Hood and others. Check www.elijahcompany.com or call (888) 235-4524.

n. **Sonlight Books**, with tons of suggestions for and descriptions of great literature; they have books from Catholic, Protestant, and non-religious perspectives. One caveat: I think they rush the age-levels. I recommend starting with lower grade level books, while holding off on the upper grade level books until your children are ready. They have an extensive website at www.sonlight.com or call (303) 730- 6292.

Happy hunting, and enjoy the books!

Permission and Acknowledgements

Permission to use copyrighted and non-copyrighted material is hereby gratefully acknowledged by the author and the Press:

Illustrations throughout the text were found in *Children: A Pictorial Archive*, selected and arranged by Carol Belanger Grafton, © 2002 and *Old-Fashioned Illustrations of Books, Reading and Writing*, selected and arranged by Carol Belanger Grafton © 1992, Dover Publications.

Quotations from *Learning All the Time*, by John Holt, © 1989, and *Teach Your Own*, by John Holt and Patrick Farenga, © 2002, republished with the kind permission of Perseus Books Group. Permission conveyed through Copyright Clearance Center, Inc.

About the Author

Suzie Andres is a graduate of Thomas Aquinas College, which she attended from 1983-1987. While there she fell in love with Jesus and the Catholic Church, the Carmelites, and Tony Andres. Suzie and Tony then attended the University of Notre Dame from 1987-1993, during which time they attended many football games, got married, and studied philosophy with Ralph McInerny. In 1990 they became the proud parents of Joseph Anthony Andres. In 1992 they entered the Secular Order of Discalced Carmelites.

In 1993 the Andres family moved to Front Royal, Virginia where Tony began teaching philosophy at Christendom College, and Suzie settled down to her life's work of enjoying her family and messing around with books. This kept her moderately busy until the birth of her second son, Dominic, who arrived in September of 2002 and immediately took over the Andres household. Suzie wrote *Homeschooling with Gentleness* in the

summer of 2003 while Dominic slept, Joseph read, and Tony studied. It is her first book, and probably her last (at least for the foreseeable future), since Dominic is beginning to exhibit all the signs of an eager and curious natural learner.